YORK PERSONAL TUTORS

Number Book 1

Garry Norman

 Longman

 York Press

YORK PERSONAL TUTORS

titles in series

GCSE English

Novels and Short Stories
Shakespeare
Film and Media
Poetry
Drama
Spelling, Grammar and Punctuation

GCSE Maths

Number Book 1
Number Book 2
Shapes, Space and Measures
Algebra
Handling Data

YORK PRESS
322 Old Brompton Road, London SW5 9JH

PEARSON EDUCATION LIMITED
Edinburgh Gate, Harlow
Essex CM20 2JE, United Kingdom
Associated companies, branches and representatives throughout the world

First published 2000

ISBN 0582 424712

Designed by Shireen Nathoo Design, London
Illustrated by Spike Gerrell
Typeset by Gem Graphics, Trenance, Mawgan Porth, Cornwall
Film output by Spectrum Colour
Printed in Great Britain by Henry Ling Limited, Dorchester, Dorset

CONTENTS

Introduction

Using numbers is as natural to us as using language. Numbers help us to make sense of, and therefore manage, the world around us. We know how to manipulate and quantify, and to predict and evaluate, so life is much easier with numbers than without them.

THINK ABOUT IT

Primitive people used numbers only when they needed to count their children, livestock, or foodstuffs. However, they used only the positive whole numbers (1,2,3 etc.). They would not have needed to use 'complicated' numbers like fractions or negative numbers. When you look at the types of calculation we do today, mathematics has developed a lot since prehistoric times!

It is very important to be able to estimate the answer to a complicated sum before actually working it out. If you can do this, you'll be able to avoid making simple mistakes, and you'll find that you'll gain a good understanding of how numbers work. You'll learn this skill as you work through this book, and through Personal Tutor Number Book 2.

DID YOU KNOW?
Although different languages have different words for 'one', 'two', 'three' etc., there is a tribe in South America whose language does not have these words. They simply have a word for 'one' and another word for 'more than one'. This means that there is no difference between, say, seven llamas and eight llamas – they are both 'more than one' llama!

This book helps you with the number work that the National Curriculum requires you to tackle for GCSE and Key Stage 3 SATs. Foundation and Intermediate tiers at GCSE require you to understand fully all the topics in this book. If you are anticipating going in for Intermediate and Higher tier GCSE, you'll need to develop your skills further with Personal Tutor Number Book 2.

There are three possible ways of using this book to help you with your coursework and exams:

1. You can work through the book from start to finish, chapter by chapter. The book has been set out in a logical sequence to make this possible.

2. If there are particular topics you want to focus on or revise, you can look up just that chapter, or series of chapters which deal with that area. This is especially useful if you want to revise a topic you are currently studying at school.

3. The Key Concepts give you concise pieces of information that you need to know for a particular topic – useful for rapid revision just before the exam.

Throughout Personal Tutor Number Book 1, the emphasis is on helping you to build up an understanding of why things work and how mathematics can be used every day, rather than just a series of rules to be learned in isolation. As you work through the book, we hope you'll find that numbers can be fun, and essential in everyday life.

THINK ABOUT IT

The number zero does occur 'naturally' as a counting number, and it was probably first used in India. The word zero comes from the Arabic 'sifr' meaning 'empty' and we get our English word 'cipher' from this too.

| N1 | Strategies | N1 |

We can use various strategies to break difficult sums down into a number of easier stages.

✳ Multiplying by 2, 4, 8, 16 and so on

Some people find it easy to **double** a number because the two times table is an easy one to remember. If we wish though, we can double a number by **adding it to itself**.

EXAMPLE

516×2 can be found by adding 516 to itself.

$$\begin{array}{r} 516 \\ + \ 516 \\ \hline 1032 \\ {\scriptstyle 1} \ \ {\scriptstyle 1} \end{array}$$

$516 \times 2 = 1032$

We can use doubling to multiply by higher numbers too. Multiplying by 4 means doubling and then doubling again. Similarly, multiplying by 8 means doubling and then doubling again to get 4 times the number and then doubling again to get 8 times the number.

EXAMPLE

Find 31×8.

Doubling 31 gives 62,
doubling again gives 124,
and doubling yet again gives 248.

$31 \times 8 = 248$

| N | O | T | E | S |

Multiplying by 5

Five is half of 10 so to multiply by 5 we can multiply by 10 and then halve the answer.

EXAMPLE   Find 234×5.

$$234 \times 10 = 2340$$
$$2340 \div 2 = 1170$$

So $234 \times 5 = 1170$

'Near misses'

Sometimes we have to deal with numbers that are very close to other numbers that would be easier to deal with.

EXAMPLE   Consider 498×3.

The value 498 is very near to 500 – we could call it a 'near miss'. The sum 500×3 is much easier to work out; it is 1500. But 498 is 2 less than 500, so the answer to our original sum will be 3×2 (three lots of 2) less than 1500. So the answer is $1500 - 6 = 1494$.

EXAMPLE   Find 301×7.

Estimate this as 300×7, which is 2100. To get the final answer we need to amend our estimate (which was **too low**) by **adding on** 1×7,

giving $2100 + 7 = 2107$.

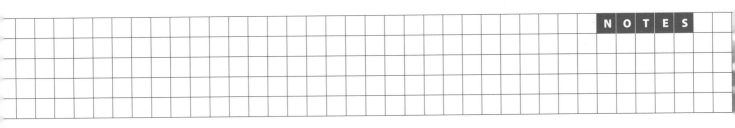

✳ Subtraction

Shopkeepers often have to calculate subtraction sums. For example when a customer offers a large bank note to pay for a small item the shopkeeper has to subtract the cost of the item from the value of the bank note. Shopkeepers use a method of 'making up' the amounts in stages.

EXAMPLE   Find 317 – 83.

First we make the 83 up to the next **ten**, which is 90.

This requires   7

Next, we make the 90 up to the next **hundred**, which is 100.

This requires   10

Next, we make the 100 up to 300.

This requires   200

Finally, we make the 300 up to 317.

This requires   <u>17</u>

Now add up these amounts to get the answer   234

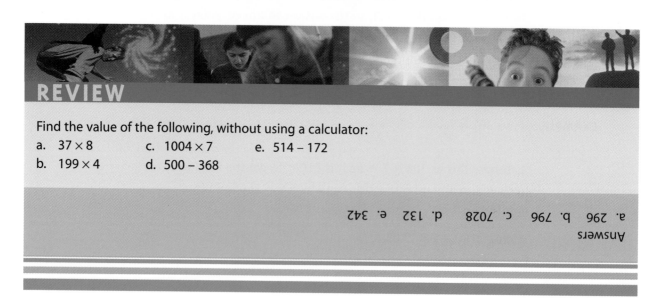

REVIEW

Find the value of the following, without using a calculator:
a.   37 × 8
b.   199 × 4
c.   1004 × 7
d.   500 – 368
e.   514 – 172

Answers

a. 296 b. 796 c. 7028 d. 132 e. 342

N2 Order of Operations N2

Lucy and Pepe were asked to do the sum '$4 + 3 \times 5$'.
Lucy said '35' and Pepe said '19'. Which answer is right?

Can you see how each of them got their answer? What answer would you have given? Who do you think was correct?

To help us obtain the right answer we have rules about the order in which to do the calculations. In the question above, Lucy did the '$4 + 3$' part first but Pepe did '3×5' first.

To get the correct answer we should **do multiplication before we do addition**, so Pepe was correct. Lucy was just working from left to right to work out the sum, whereas Pepe knew that we always do multiplying before adding.

Multiplying is a **higher order operation** than adding, so we do it first. Subtracting is at the same level as adding so, again, multiplying would come first.

> *MULTIPLYING IS A HIGHER ORDER OPERATION THAN ADDING*

EXAMPLE $4 \times 5 - 3 = 17$ and $13 - 2 \times 4 = 5$

Dividing is at the same level as multiplying so dividing should be done before any adding or subtracting. If we have two operations at the same level then to decide which is to be done first we simply do the ones on the left first.

EXAMPLE

	$5 \times 2 + 3 \times 1$	we do the '5×2' first (leftmost multiplication)
which gives	$10 + 3 \times 1$	now we do '3×1' (multiplying before adding)
which gives	$10 + 3$	
which is	13	

Can you see that $9 + 28 \div 4 - 2 \times 3 + 5 = 15$?

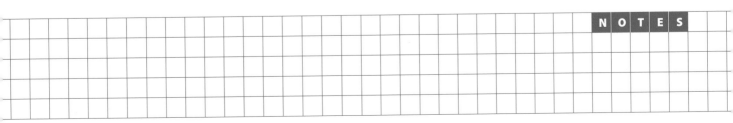

It is possible to force a sum to be calculated in a different order by using brackets.

Brackets always mean 'do this before anything else'. Putting brackets in the sum above changes the final answer.

BRACKETS ALWAYS MEAN 'DO THIS BEFORE ANYTHING ELSE'.

EXAMPLE

$9 + 28 \div (4 - 2) \times 3 + 5$	using brackets forces '4 − 2' to be calculated first
$9 + 28 \div 2 \times 3 + 5$	working from left to right, ÷ must be done first
$9 + 14 \times 3 + 5$	working from left to right, × must be done next
$9 + 42 + 5$	now we only have + to do
56	

So the correct order of operations is Brackets, Divide, Multiply, Add, Subtract. Think of a word or phrase to help you to remember it. Some people use **BODMAS**. How about Blanket Dust Might Attract Spiders?

Divide and Multiply are of equal priority, but higher than Add and Subtract, which are also of equal priority.

THE CORRECT ORDER OF OPERATIONS IS BRACKETS, DIVIDE, MULTIPLY, ADD, SUBTRACT.

THINK ABOUT IT

By using brackets in different places just one set of numbers and operations can produce many different answers.

For example, from $12 - 4 \div 2 + 1$ we could make:

$$11 = 12 - (4 \div 2) + 1$$
$$5 = (12 - 4) \div 2 + 1$$
$$9 = 12 - (4 \div 2 + 1)$$

N	O	T	E	S

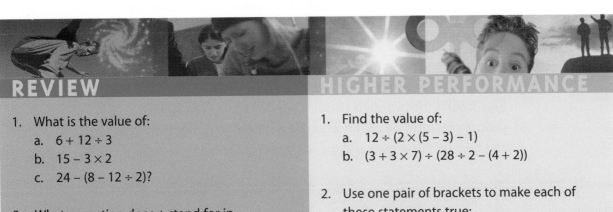

REVIEW

1. What is the value of:
   a. $6 + 12 \div 3$
   b. $15 - 3 \times 2$
   c. $24 - (8 - 12 \div 2)$?

2. What operation does * stand for in the sums:
   a. $5 * 3 + 2 = 17$
   b. $7 - 12 * 2 = 1$
   c. $6 * (8 \times 5 - 8) = 38$

Answers

1. a. 10   b. 9   c. 22
2. a. ×   b. ÷   c. +

HIGHER PERFORMANCE

1. Find the value of:
   a. $12 \div (2 \times (5 - 3) - 1)$
   b. $(3 + 3 \times 7) \div (28 \div 2 - (4 + 2))$

2. Use one pair of brackets to make each of these statements true:
   a. $5 + 3 - 2 = 6$
   b. $30 - 6 + 4 \times 2 = 16$
   c. $30 - 6 \div 4 \times 2 = 12$

Answers

1. a. 4   b. 3
2. a. $(5 + 3) - 2 = 6$
   b. $30 - (6 + 4 \times 2) = 16$
   c. $(30 - 6) \div 4 \times 2 = 12$

N O T E S

| N3 | ## Multiplication of Whole Numbers by Two-digit Numbers | N3 |

Numbers are made up from digits. The number 403 is made up from the digits 4, 0 and 3. Two-digit numbers are the numbers from 10 to 99. They use two digits: one in the units column and one in the tens column.

When we multiply a number by another two-digit number we have to split the two-digit number into the units digit and the tens digit. To multiply by 26, for example, we need to multiply by 20 and then by 6 and then add the two results together.

EXAMPLE The calculation would be set out like this.

write 638×26 like this:

$$\begin{array}{r} 638 \\ \times\ 26 \\ \hline \end{array}$$

First we multiply by the units digit, 6. Work along the number, multiplying by the units digit, 6.

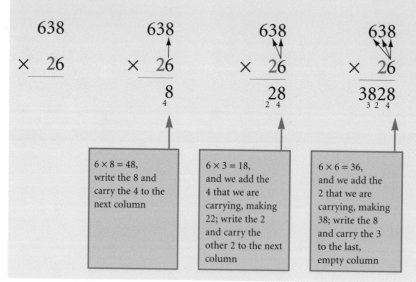

| $6 \times 8 = 48$, write the 8 and carry the 4 to the next column | $6 \times 3 = 18$, and we add the 4 that we are carrying, making 22; write the 2 and carry the other 2 to the next column | $6 \times 6 = 36$, and we add the 2 that we are carrying, making 38; write the 8 and carry the 3 to the last, empty column |

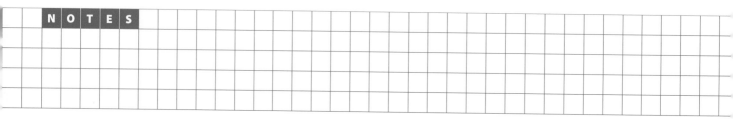

We now have to multiply by the tens digit, that is the 2. This is, in effect, multiplying by 20 and the easiest way to do this is to write down a zero and then write down the result of multiplying by 2.

We write this second part underneath the first part so that the two parts will be lined up for adding at the end.

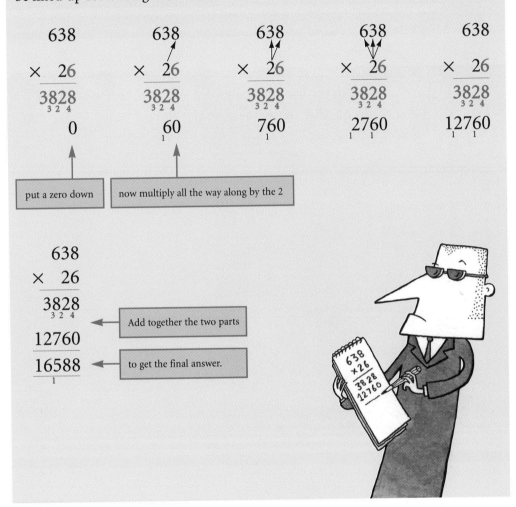

When you do a sum like this it is always a good idea to estimate what the answer should be and compare this with the answer that you get. In the example above we could say that 638 is approximately 600 and that 26 is approximately 20 or 30. So our answer could be, roughly, 600×20, which is $12\,000$, or 600×30, which is $18\,000$. The answer that we found came out between these two values.

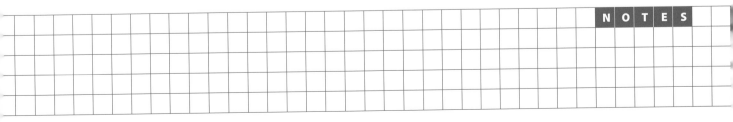

KEY CONCEPTS

✳ Numbers are made up from digits

✳ To multiply by a two-digit number we multiply first by the units digit

✳ Then, by putting down a zero first, multiply by the tens digit

✳ Then add these two results together to get the final answer

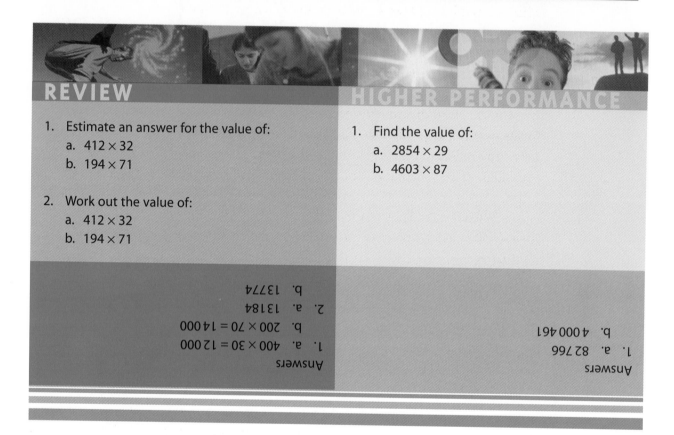

REVIEW

1. Estimate an answer for the value of:
   a. 412×32
   b. 194×71

2. Work out the value of:
   a. 412×32
   b. 194×71

Answers
1. a. $400 \times 30 = 12\,000$
   b. $200 \times 70 = 14\,000$
2. a. 13184
   b. 13774

HIGHER PERFORMANCE

1. Find the value of:
   a. 2854×29
   b. 4603×87

Answers
1. a. $82\,766$
   b. $4\,000\,461$

N4 — Division of Whole Numbers by Two-digit Numbers

When we have to divide a number by a two-digit number we need to use a times table that we do not, usually, learn. For example, when we divide by 7 we use the seven times table, but when we divide by 29 we would need to use the twenty-nine times table and nobody would expect us to have learned that!

However even though we do not have to remember the twenty-nine times table we would need to work out some of the table as we work through the division.

You will recall that in division sums, where we have to divide by just a single digit (such as dividing by 7), we 'carry over' remainders to the next column and we write the 'carry over' digit very small and in front of the digit in the next column. When we are dealing with much larger numbers, as we are when we divide by numbers like 29, there is often not the room to write 'carry over' numbers so we use a different method of 'bringing down' the next column digit.

EXAMPLE

First of all we set out the sum $7337 \div 29$ like this: $29\overline{)7337}$

The first question we ask ourselves is 'How many times does 29 go into 7?' The answer is 'None!'

This means that we now use the digit in the second column and ask 'How many times does 29 go into 73?' I do not know my twenty-nine times table so I need to start working it out to answer this question.

$29 \times 1 = 29$ That was easy!

$29 \times 2 = 58$ Just double the 'one times' answer above. We still have not reached 73, so carry on.

$29 \times 3 = 87$ Add the one times answer to the two times answer.

Now we have gone past 73 so we can stop working out the twenty-nine times table.

The answer to 'How many times does 29 go into 73?' is 'Twice, with some left over'. Write the answer '2', above the '3' on the answer line. We are not going to work out how much is left over in our heads. Instead, we will perform a subtraction sum to show 73 minus 58.

Our sum now looks like this:

$$\begin{array}{r} 2 \\ 29\overline{)7337} \\ -\,58 \end{array}$$

Doing the subtraction gives:

$$\begin{array}{r} 2 \\ 29\overline{)7337} \\ -\,58 \\ \hline 15 \end{array}$$

At this point, remember that we do not write the 'carry over' number (15 in this case) in small print but instead we 'bring down' the next column digit and write it next to the 'carry over' number.

$$\begin{array}{r} 2 \\ 29\overline{)7337} \\ -\,58\!\downarrow \\ \hline 153 \end{array}$$

Now we ask the question 'How many times does 29 go into 153?' Look at the twenty-nine times table that we started earlier. It only went up to 87 so we have to work out some more of the table (but no more than we absolutely have to!). Our sum now looks like this:

$29 \times 1 = 29$
$29 \times 2 = 58$
$29 \times 3 = 87$
$29 \times 4 = 116$ Just double the two times answer. We are not past 153 yet, so carry on.
$29 \times 5 = 145$ Just add the two times answer to the three times answer. We are not past 153 yet, so carry on.
$29 \times 6 = 174$ Just double the three times answer. This is more than 153, so the answer to 'How many times does 29 go into 153?' is 'Five times with some left over'

Our sum now looks like this:

$$
\begin{array}{r}
25 \\
29\overline{)7337} \\
-\,58\!\downarrow \\
\hline
153 \\
\end{array}
$$

do the subtraction:

$$
\begin{array}{r}
153 \\
-\,145 \\
\hline
8 \\
\end{array}
$$

$$
\begin{array}{r}
25 \\
29\overline{)7337} \\
-\,58\!\downarrow \\
\hline
153 \\
-\,145\!\downarrow \\
\hline
\end{array}
$$

bring down the 7: $\quad 87$

Now we need to ask the question 'How many times does 29 go into 87?' Thankfully we do not need to do any more working out as we already have the answer in our twenty-nine times table so far. Look at the working out that we did earlier and we can see that 29 goes into 87 exactly three times.

Finally, then, our sum looks like this:

$$
\begin{array}{r}
253 \\
29\overline{)7337} \\
-\,58\!\downarrow \\
\hline
153 \\
-\,145\!\downarrow \\
\hline
87 \\
\end{array}
$$

$$7337 \div 29 = 253$$

DID YOU KNOW?

We can sometimes make two-digit division easier by splitting the sum into two easier sums. For example, dividing by the number 24 is the same as dividing by 6 and then dividing by 4 (both of these sums use times tables that we know).

Similarly, we can divide by 20 by dividing by 10 and then dividing by 2.

KEY CONCEPTS

✳ Work out a times table in easy stages, only finding the numbers that you have to

✳ Extend your times table by looking at earlier answers and using them to find other values

✳ Do not 'carry over' but, instead, 'bring down'

✳ If the number does not go in, put a zero down in the answer line

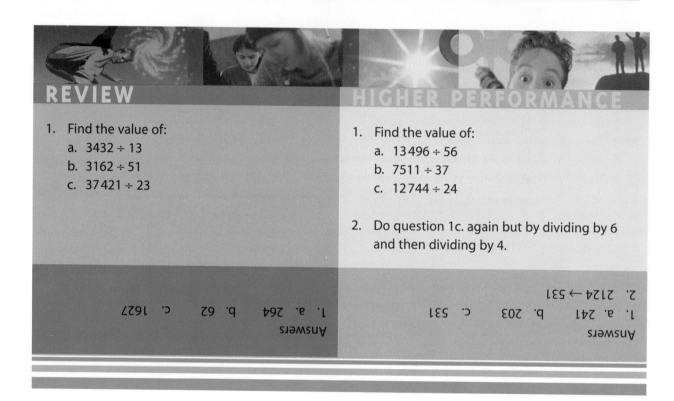

REVIEW

1. Find the value of:
   a. 3432 ÷ 13
   b. 3162 ÷ 51
   c. 37421 ÷ 23

HIGHER PERFORMANCE

1. Find the value of:
   a. 13496 ÷ 56
   b. 7511 ÷ 37
   c. 12744 ÷ 24

2. Do question 1c. again but by dividing by 6 and then dividing by 4.

Answers

1. a. 264 b. 62 c. 1627

Answers

1. a. 241 b. 203 c. 531

2. 2124 → 531

N5	Multiples, Factors and Prime Numbers	N5

Multiples

Multiples of a number are what you get when you multiply the number by 1, 2, 3, 4, and so on.

> THINK OF 'MULTIPLES OF' MEANING 'MULTIPLY BY'

EXAMPLE

12 is the third multiple of 4

12 is the fourth multiple of 3

12 is the first multiple of 12

but 12 is **not** a multiple of 7 and 12 is **not** a multiple of 24.

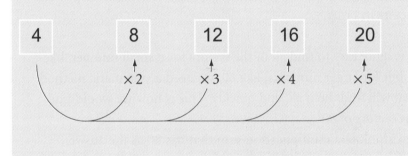

The numbers in the boxes are all multiples of 4.

DID YOU KNOW?

All the multiples of an even number are also even numbers but the multiples of an odd number can be odd or even numbers.

N O T E S

✳ Factors

FACTORS OF A NUMBER DIVIDE EXACTLY INTO THE NUMBER

Factors of a number are the numbers that divide exactly into the number.

EXAMPLE   Let's think of all the numbers that go into 8 exactly.

| 2 | 8 | 1 |

Can you think of any other factors of 8?

We say that the factors of 8 are {1, 2, 4, 8}. It is useful to put the factors in order.

It is quite easy to find all of the factors for a small number, like 8, but for larger numbers, like 80, we need a systematic method that will find them all, and quickly. This is how we would find the factors of 80.

Think of a multiplication sum that has 80 as the answer, such as '40 × 2 = 80'. This gives us two factors of 80 straight away. They are 2 and 40. This is a good method, but a bit 'hit-and-miss', so we should now be systematic and search for numbers that divide into 80, in order, and every time that we find **one** we will have **another** one at the same time! Always start with 1 because it's guaranteed to give you a pair of factors: 1 × 80 = 80. Now write down 1, and its partner 80.

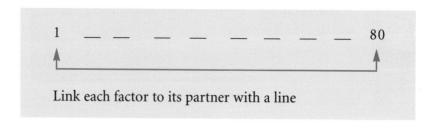

Link each factor to its partner with a line

We are on our way! We have two of the factors.

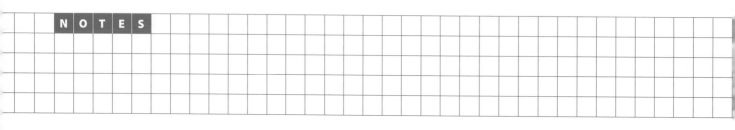

After 1, try 2. Does 2 divide into 80?

Yes! We have already said that '80 = 40 × 2'.

This gives us another pair of factors. Add them to your diagram.

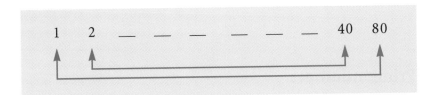

Notice that we do not have to search for any numbers between 40 and 80 that divide into 80 because our diagram shows that there is no room for a partner of such number between 1 and 2.

Next, we should try 3, but 3 does not divide exactly into 80 so we try 4. Eventually we have a diagram like this:

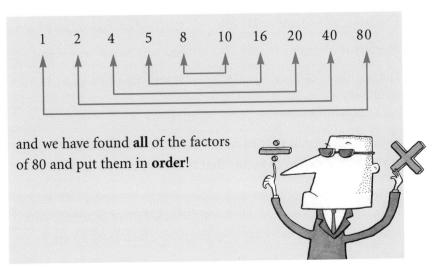

and we have found **all** of the factors of 80 and put them in **order**!

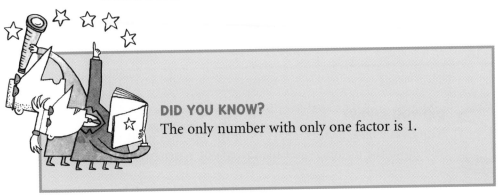

DID YOU KNOW?
The only number with only one factor is 1.

THINK ABOUT IT

What kind of numbers have an **odd** number of factors?

Answer: square numbers

✳ Prime numbers

Numbers which have **two, and only two,** factors are called
prime numbers. Their factors are always themselves and 1.

> THE FACTORS OF PRIME NUMBERS ARE ALWAYS THE NUMBER AND 1

EXAMPLE

The factors of 13 are	{1, 13}	exactly two factors so 13 is a prime number
The factors of 9 are	{1, 3, 9}	three factors so 9 is **not** a prime number
The factors of 23 are	{1, 23}	exactly two factors so 23 is a prime number
The factor of 1 is	{1}	just one factor so 1 is **not** a prime number
The factors of 167 are	{1, 167}	exactly two factors so 167 is a prime number

Another important type of number is a prime factor. This is,
as you would expect, a **factor that is also a prime number**.

> A PRIME FACTOR IS A FACTOR THAT IS ALSO A PRIME NUMBER

EXAMPLE

The factors of 18 are 1, 2, 3, 6, 9 and 18. Of these factors, 2 and
3 are also primes, so we say that the prime factors of 18 are 2
and 3.

DID YOU KNOW?
Numbers whose factors, apart from the number itself,
add up to the number are called **perfect numbers**

KEY CONCEPTS

A multiple of a number is the number you get when you multiply it by another number ✳

Factors of a number are those numbers that divide exactly into that number ✳

Prime numbers are numbers with two and only two factors: themselves and 1 ✳

REVIEW

1. Find the multiples of 6 that are less than 50.

2. Add the third multiple of 12 to the fifth multiple of 11.

3. Find all of the factors of 24.

4. Find the prime factors of 350.

5. Which of these numbers are prime numbers: 15, 49, 29, 39?

Answers

1. 6, 12, 18, 24, 30, 36, 42, 48
2. 36 + 55 = 91
3. 1, 2, 3, 4, 6, 8, 12, 24
4. 2, 5, 7
5. only 29

HIGHER PERFORMANCE

1. Which multiples of 4 are also factors of 48?

2. Which is greater, the fifth multiple of 7 or the seventh multiple of 5?

3. Find a number, less than 100, that is a multiple of 5 and has eight factors.

4. Find the factors of 6. Add them up (except for 6 itself). You should get the answer '6', the original number. Find the next perfect number after 6.

Answers

1. 4, 8, 12, 16, 24, 48
2. they are the same
3. 30 or 40 or 70
4. 28

Squares, Cubes and Higher Powers

Multiplying a number by itself is called **squaring**. The result is called the **square** of the number.

A shorthand way of writing 'squared' is as a little '2' after the number, like this: 7^2. The two is called the **power** and we say '7 raised to the power of 2 is 49'.

So the sum '$7 \times 7 = 49$' can be written and described in several ways.

> MULTIPLYING A NUMBER BY ITSELF IS CALLED SQUARING

EXAMPLE

$7^2 = 49$	squaring 7 gives 49
7 squared is 49	the square of 7 is 49
$7 \times 7 = 49$	7 to the power of 2 is 49

If we multiply a number by itself and then by itself **again**, then we have **cubed** the number.

EXAMPLE

$7^3 = 343$	cubing 7 gives 343
7 cubed is 343	the cube of 7 is 343
$7 \times 7 \times 7 = 343$	7 to the power of 3 is 343

We have no special names (such as squaring and cubing) for multiplying a number by itself more than three times, but we can still use the power notation.

EXAMPLE $2^5 = $ '2 to the power of 5' $= 2 \times 2 \times 2 \times 2 \times 2 = 32$

NOTES

THINK ABOUT IT

There are two numbers that stay the same no matter what power they are raised to. What are they?

Answer: 0 and 1

KEY CONCEPTS

✳ Raising a number to a power means repeatedly multiplying the number by itself

✳ Squaring means raising a number to the power of 2

✳ Cubing means raising a number to the power of 3

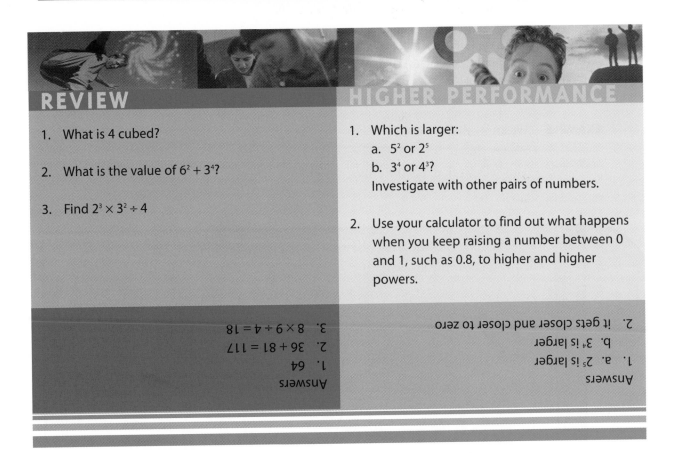

REVIEW

1. What is 4 cubed?

2. What is the value of $6^2 + 3^4$?

3. Find $2^3 \times 3^2 \div 4$

HIGHER PERFORMANCE

1. Which is larger:
   a. 5^2 or 2^5
   b. 3^4 or 4^3?
   Investigate with other pairs of numbers.

2. Use your calculator to find out what happens when you keep raising a number between 0 and 1, such as 0.8, to higher and higher powers.

Answers
1. 64
2. 36 + 81 = 117
3. 8 × 9 ÷ 4 = 18

Answers
1. a. 2^5 is larger
   b. 3^4 is larger
2. it gets closer and closer to zero

Square Roots and Cube Roots

In N6, Squares, Cubes and Higher Powers, we dealt with squaring and cubing numbers. This section is about the reverse operations of finding a square root or cube root of a number.

To find the **square root** of a number we are looking for the number that we have to square (that is, multiply by itself) in order to get the original number.

EXAMPLE

We know that $6^2 = 36$.
We say this as 'six squared is equal to thirty-six'.
This tells us that 6 is the square root of 36.

Similarly, the **cube root** of a number is the number that we have to cube in order to get the original number.

EXAMPLE

We know that $4^3 = 64$.
We say this as 'four cubed is equal to sixty-four'.
This tells us that 4 is the cube root of 64.

THINK ABOUT IT

It's like finding the 'squaring question' or 'cubing question' when you know the answer!

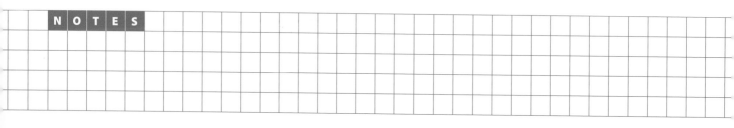

N O T E S

In mathematics we have a special symbol for square root or cube root. It is called a 'root sign' and looks like $\sqrt{}$ for a square root and $\sqrt[3]{}$ for a cube root.

EXAMPLE Using these symbols we can write:

$$\sqrt{49} = 7 \quad \text{and} \quad \sqrt[3]{125} = 5$$

Find the keys on your calculator that do these operations. There is usually one key for square roots (with the $\sqrt{}$ symbol on it) and another key (with a $\sqrt[n]{}$ or $\sqrt[3]{}$ symbol on it) for cube roots. You will need to read the instruction manual for your calculator.

WE NEED TO USE A CALCULATOR FOR MOST SQUARE AND CUBE ROOTS

Check these on your calculator:

$$\sqrt{20} = 4.472\ldots \quad \text{and} \quad \sqrt[3]{17} = 2.571\ldots$$

DID YOU KNOW?
If you choose a number and then find its square root and then square the answer, you get the original number.

KEY CONCEPTS

The square root of a number is the number that you have to square to get the original number ✳

The cube root of a number is the number that you have to cube to get the original number ✳

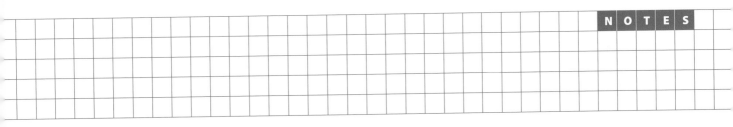

N O T E S

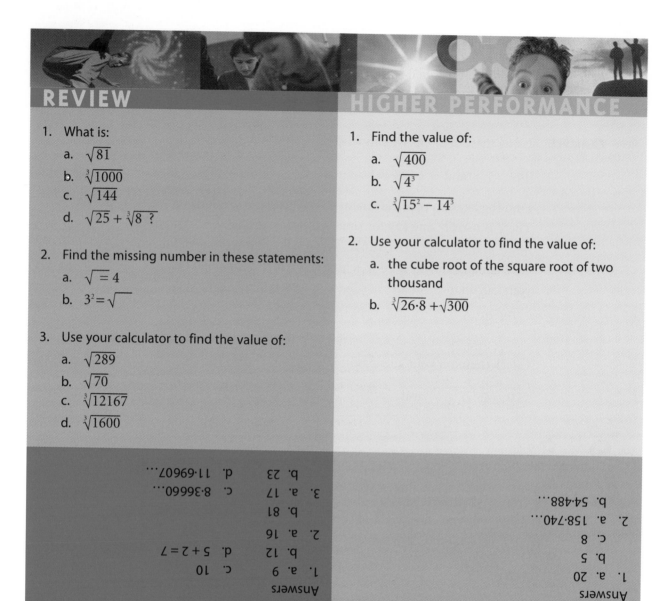

REVIEW

1. What is:
   a. $\sqrt{81}$
   b. $\sqrt[3]{1000}$
   c. $\sqrt{144}$
   d. $\sqrt{25} + \sqrt[3]{8}$?

2. Find the missing number in these statements:
   a. $\sqrt{} = 4$
   b. $3^2 = \sqrt{}$

3. Use your calculator to find the value of:
   a. $\sqrt{289}$
   b. $\sqrt{70}$
   c. $\sqrt[3]{12167}$
   d. $\sqrt[3]{1600}$

HIGHER PERFORMANCE

1. Find the value of:
   a. $\sqrt{400}$
   b. $\sqrt{4^3}$
   c. $\sqrt[3]{15^2 - 14^3}$

2. Use your calculator to find the value of:
   a. the cube root of the square root of two thousand
   b. $\sqrt[3]{26 \cdot 8} + \sqrt{300}$

Answers

1. a. 9   c. 10
   d. 5 + 2 = 7
   b. 12
2. a. 16
   b. 81
3. a. 17   c. 8·36660...
   b. 23   d. 11·69607...

Answers

1. a. 20
   b. 5
   c. 8
2. a. 158·740...
   b. 54·488...

N8 | Equivalent Fractions | **N8**

Ayesha is treating her friends to a pizza. She has cut the pizza into **twelve** equal pieces. Each piece is a **twelfth** of a pizza, that is $\frac{1}{12}$.

Ayesha's friends are calling in to see her but she does not know how many will arrive.

If three people share the pizza then they would each have $\frac{1}{3}$ (one-third) of the pizza.	If six people share the pizza then they would each have $\frac{1}{6}$ (one-sixth) of the pizza.	If four people share the pizza then they would each have $\frac{1}{4}$ (one-quarter) of the pizza.
Each of the three people would have four slices, that is four of the twelfths, so one-third equals four-twelfths:	Each of the six people would have two slices, that is two of the twelfths, so one-sixth equals two-twelfths:	Each of the four people would have three slices, so one-quarter equals three-twelfths:
$$\frac{1}{3} = \frac{4}{12}$$	$$\frac{1}{6} = \frac{2}{12}$$	$$\frac{1}{4} = \frac{3}{12}$$
We call $\frac{1}{3}$ and $\frac{4}{12}$ equivalent fractions – they stand for the same amount.	So $\frac{1}{6}$ and $\frac{2}{12}$ are equivalent fractions.	So $\frac{1}{4}$ and $\frac{3}{12}$ are equivalent fractions.

EQUIVALENT FRACTIONS STAND FOR THE SAME AMOUNT

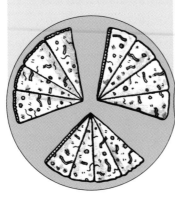  

NOTES

There is a link between equivalent fractions. As long as we multiply, or divide, both the top (**numerator**) and bottom (**denominator**) of a fraction by the **same number** we will make a new but equivalent fraction.

EXAMPLE

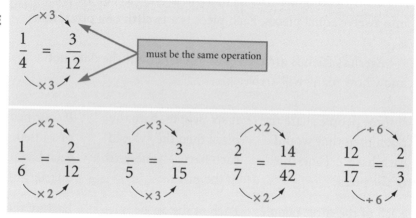

✳ Simplest form

We can sometimes **simplify** a fraction if we can find a number that divides into both the top (numerator) and bottom (denominator), like dividing by 6 as in one of the examples above. A fraction is in its **simplest form** if it is expressed using the smallest possible numbers. That is, there is no number (apart from 1) that divides into both the top (numerator) and bottom (denominator).

> A FRACTION IN ITS SIMPLEST FORM USES THE SMALLEST POSSIBLE NUMBERS

We can achieve this in several steps – we do not have to do it in only one step. For example, if we want to give $\frac{216}{360}$ in its simplest form we might not spot straight away that 72 divides into both the top (numerator) and bottom (denominator) to give us the answer $\frac{3}{5}$. However, we can achieve the same result by dividing by smaller numbers in several steps.

EXAMPLE

$$\frac{216}{360} = \frac{108}{180} = \frac{54}{90} = \frac{18}{30} = \frac{6}{10} = \frac{3}{5}$$

NOTES

KEY CONCEPTS

Multiplying the top and bottom of a fraction by the same number produces an equivalent fraction ✳

Dividing the top and bottom of a fraction by the same number produces an equivalent fraction ✳

A fraction is in its simplest form if it is expressed using the smallest possible numbers ✳

DID YOU KNOW?
If one of the numbers in a fraction is 1 or both numbers are prime numbers then it is already in its simplest form.

REVIEW

1. Find the missing number in these equivalent fractions:

   a. $\frac{1}{4} = \frac{*}{20}$ b. $\frac{5}{10} = \frac{1}{*}$

   c. $\frac{*}{3} = \frac{16}{24}$ d. $\frac{5}{*} = \frac{20}{24}$

2. Write these fractions in theair simplest form:

   a. $\frac{15}{30}$ b. $\frac{75}{100}$ c. $\frac{40}{60}$ d. $\frac{250}{400}$

Answers

1. a. $\frac{1}{4} = \frac{5}{20}$ b. $\frac{5}{10} = \frac{1}{2}$ c. $\frac{2}{3} = \frac{16}{24}$ d. $\frac{5}{6} = \frac{20}{24}$

2. a. $\frac{1}{2}$ b. $\frac{3}{4}$ c. $\frac{2}{3}$ d. $\frac{5}{8}$

HIGHER PERFORMANCE

1. Find the missing numbers:

   a. $\frac{6}{*} = \frac{*}{14} = \frac{18}{21}$ b. $\frac{16}{*} = \frac{2}{9} = \frac{*}{36}$

Answers

1. a. $\frac{6}{7} = \frac{12}{14} = \frac{18}{21}$ b. $\frac{16}{72} = \frac{2}{9} = \frac{8}{36}$

N9   Introduction to Percentages   N9

The word **percentage** means 'a fraction with a denominator (bottom number) of 100'.

    A percentage is a fraction of 100.

EXAMPLE   74% means $\dfrac{74}{100}$

> A PERCENTAGE IS A FRACTION OF 100

Percentages are particularly helpful when we want to compare fractions.

EXAMPLE In a French test Luke scored 17 out of 20. In the German test there was a total of 50 marks and Luke scored 42. Did he do better in French or German?

Luke's scores, written as fractions, are:

French $\dfrac{17}{20}$ and German $\dfrac{42}{50}$

In N8, Equivalent Fractions, we saw how to find equivalent fractions. What is needed here is to make each of these fractions into fractions of 100; that is, percentages.

$$\overset{\times 5}{\underset{\times 5}{\dfrac{17}{20}}} = \dfrac{85}{100} = 85\% \text{ for French} \qquad \overset{\times 2}{\underset{\times 2}{\dfrac{42}{50}}} = \dfrac{84}{100} = 84\% \text{ for German}$$

Luke did better in French.

N O T E S

Some fractions and percentages occur often and should be **remembered**. They also help when we are estimating.

$\dfrac{1}{4} = \dfrac{25}{100} = 25\%$	$\dfrac{1}{2} = \dfrac{50}{100} = 50\%$	$\dfrac{3}{4} = \dfrac{75}{100} = 75\%$	$1 = \dfrac{100}{100} = 100\%$
$\dfrac{1}{10} = \dfrac{10}{100} = 10\%$	$\dfrac{2}{10} = \dfrac{20}{100} = 20\%$	$\dfrac{3}{10} = \dfrac{30}{100} = 30\%$	and so on…

KEY CONCEPTS

Percentages are fractions with denominators of 100 ✻

To convert a fraction to a percentage we have to find the equivalent fraction of 100 ✻

Some percentage equivalents of fractions occur frequently and should be remembered ✻

REVIEW

1. Write these fractions as percentages:

   a. $\dfrac{7}{10}$ b. $\dfrac{1}{5}$ c. $\dfrac{4}{5}$ d. $\dfrac{18}{50}$ e. $\dfrac{7}{25}$

2. In his first science test Luke scored 16 out of 25. In the second science test he scored 13 out of 20. Did Luke improve or get worse in science, and by how many percent?

Answers

1. a. 70%   b. 20%   c. 80%
   d. 36%   e. 28%

2. first test = 64%, second test = 65%, so he improved by 1%

HIGHER PERFORMANCE

1. Put these sets of three quantities in order from smallest to largest:

   a. $\dfrac{18}{25}$, 70% , $\dfrac{3}{4}$

   b. 19% , $\dfrac{2}{5}$, one-quarter

2. Convert these percentages to decimals:

   a. 12·5%   b. 0·7%

Answers

a. 70%, $\dfrac{18}{25}$, $\dfrac{3}{4}$

b. 19%, one-quarter, $\dfrac{2}{5}$

N O T E S

N10 Introduction to Decimal Fractions N10

The decimal system is a place value system in that the positions (or placing) of the digits of a whole number tell us the numbers of units, tens, hundreds, thousands, and so on, that make up that number. Similarly, the positions of the digits of a fraction less than 1 written using the decimal system tell us the numbers of tenths, hundredths, thousandths, and so on, that make up that fraction.

The positions of the digits, or places, look like this:

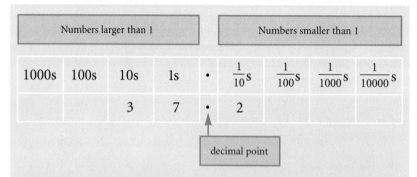

Numbers larger than 1					Numbers smaller than 1			
1000s	100s	10s	1s	•	$\frac{1}{10}$s	$\frac{1}{100}$s	$\frac{1}{1000}$s	$\frac{1}{10000}$s
		3	7	•	2			

decimal point

'37·2' stands for three tens, seven units and two tenths, which we say as 'thirty-seven point two'.

1000s	100s	10s	1s	•	$\frac{1}{10}$s	$\frac{1}{100}$s	$\frac{1}{1000}$s	$\frac{1}{10000}$s
	8	0	4	•	5	9		

'804·59' stands for eight hundreds, no tens, four units, five tenths and nine hundredths, which we say as 'eight hundred and four point five nine'.

Inserting zeros in some places affects the value of the number, but inserting zeros in other places does not change the value. For example:

804·59 is not the same as **804·059** but **804·59** is the same as **804·590**

804·59 is not the same as **804·509** but **804·59** is the same as **804·590 000**

804·59 is not the same as **804·0059** but **804·59** is the same as **804·590 000 000**

To understand the value of a number correctly we need to know exactly which column each figure is in. To do this we must always make sure that the decimal point is in the correct place.

EXAMPLE Three-hundredths would be shown as:

1000s	100s	10s	1s	·	$\frac{1}{10}$s	$\frac{1}{100}$s	$\frac{1}{1000}$s	$\frac{1}{10000}$s
				·	0	3		

and written as 0·03. We usually put an extra 0 in front of the · to emphasise the decimal point. We say this number as 'nought point nought three' or 'zero point zero three'. In this number, the zero in the tenths column is needed to force the three into the correct column to show hundredths.

Some fractions take up more than one column when we write them as decimal fractions.

EXAMPLE

$$\frac{47}{1000}$$

We are unable to write both the '4' and the '7' in the $\frac{1}{1000}$ column – there is only room for one figure in each column.

But $\frac{47}{1000}$ can be split into $\frac{40}{1000}$ and $\frac{7}{1000}$. Using equivalent fractions (N8, Equivalent Fractions) we can rewrite this as:

$$\frac{47}{1000} = \frac{40}{1000} + \frac{7}{1000} = \frac{4}{100} + \frac{7}{1000} = 0{\cdot}047$$

This means that $\frac{92}{1000}$ as a decimal fraction is $0{\cdot}092$ and that $\frac{31}{100}$ as a decimal fraction is $0{\cdot}31$.

KEY CONCEPTS

✳ Decimal fractions are written using columns of tenths, hundredths, thousandths, and so on

✳ Zeros are used sometimes to place numbers into the correct columns

✳ Only one digit can appear in each column

NOTES

REVIEW

1. Write these numbers as decimal fractions:
   a. $26\frac{4}{10}$
   b. five hundred and eight and two tenths
   c. $8\frac{6}{100}$
   d. $\frac{3}{1000}$
   e. 102 and $\frac{7}{10}$ and $\frac{5}{10000}$
   f. $\frac{97}{1000}$
   g. $\frac{14}{100}$

2. Write these decimal fractions as normal fractions:
   a. 0·8   d. 0·019
   b. 0·004   e. 0·73
   c. 0·205

Answers

2. a. $\frac{8}{10} = \frac{4}{5}$ b. $\frac{4}{1000} = \frac{1}{250}$ c. $\frac{205}{1000} = \frac{41 \cdot 5}{200}$
        d. 0·003
   g. 0·14   c. 8·06
   f. 0·097   b. 508·2
   e. 102·7005   1. a. 26·4

HIGHER PERFORMANCE

1. Put these sets of three quantities in order from smallest to largest:
   a. 0·612, 0·165, 0·156
   b. 0·05, 0·1, 0·15
   c. 30·06, 3·6, 6·03
   d. 0·082, 0·8, 0·28

Answers

d. 0·082, 0·28, 0·8
c. 3·6, 6·03, 30·06
b. 0·05, 0·1, 0·15
1. a. 0·156, 0·165, 0·612

N O T E S

N11	Equivalence Between Fractions, Percentages and Decimals	N11

It is easy to compare two values if they are both in the same format; that is,

- both of them are expressed as **percentages** or
- both of them are expressed as **decimals** or
- both of them are expressed as **fractions** with the same denominator.

If they are not in the same format then we have to convert them to the same format to compare them. We could convert everything to decimals or everything to fractions or everything to percentages. Converting to a fraction is sometimes very difficult so, of these options, it is usually best to convert either to percentages or to decimals. In practice we often choose to convert to decimals.

Some conversions are easy because they are commonly known equivalences.

EXAMPLE   We know that $\frac{1}{10}$ is the same as 0·1 and also the same as 10%.

In the same way, we know that $\frac{3}{10} = 0\cdot3 = 30\%$.

 ## Converting fractions to decimals

Fractions can be turned into decimals by dividing the denominator (bottom number) into the numerator (top number).

EXAMPLE   The fraction $\frac{3}{8}$ means $3 \div 8$.

We can find this decimal value as follows: $8\overline{)3}$

When we try to divide 8 into 3 it does not go.

Show that 8 into 3 does not go by putting a zero above the 3 and 'carrying over' the 3 to the next column. We also need to put a decimal point after the 3 because we are now carrying over to the tenths column.

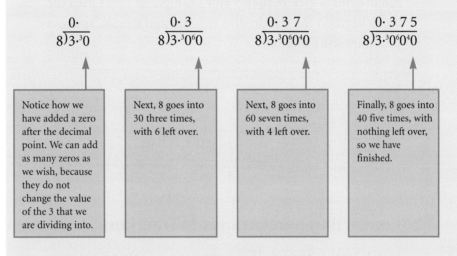

Notice how we have added a zero after the decimal point. We can add as many zeros as we wish, because they do not change the value of the 3 that we are dividing into.

Next, 8 goes into 30 three times, with 6 left over.

Next, 8 goes into 60 seven times, with 4 left over.

Finally, 8 goes into 40 five times, with nothing left over, so we have finished.

So, the fraction $\frac{3}{8}$ = the decimal quantity 0·375.

DID YOU KNOW?

Some fractions, when we turn them into decimals, do not 'finish'. They carry on for ever. For example, turn $\frac{4}{11}$ into a decimal (use your calculator to do 4 ÷ 11) to get 0·454545 45…

There is more on this in unit N41, Rational and Irrational Numbers Using Surds.

✳ Converting percentages to decimals

Remember that percentages are fractions with denominators of 100, so any percentage can be written as the same number of hundredths. So, for example, 7% = 0·07. If the number of hundredths is greater than 9 (for example in 17%) then the digits begin in the hundredths column and simply 'spill over' into the tenths column.

EXAMPLE   This means that:

43% = 0·43

60% = 0·60 (which we could write as 0·6)

$120\% = \frac{120}{100} = 1·20$ (which we could write as 1·2)

✳ Converting percentages to fractions

In N9, Introduction to Percentages, we saw that percentages are fractions with denominators of 100. This means that converting a percentage to a fraction is very easy because every percent is a hundredth.

EXAMPLE $43\% = \frac{43}{100}$

Sometimes we can simplify the fraction, as we did in N8, Equivalent Fractions.

EXAMPLE $35\% = \frac{35}{100} = \frac{7}{20}$

Converting decimals to fractions

In N10, Introduction to Decimal Fractions, we saw that decimals are written in terms of tenths, hundredths and so on. This means that some decimals can be written as fractions very easily.

EXAMPLE

$0.4 = \frac{4}{10}$

$0.008 = \frac{8}{1000}$

But if we have several digits it becomes a little more complicated. Look at the example above where it shows $35\% = \frac{35}{100}$. Using the decimal columns we begin to write '35' in the hundredths column and, because '35' consists of two digits, the 3 spills over into the tenths column, like this: 0·35. So the decimal 0·35 as a fraction is $\frac{35}{100}$, which can be simplified (as in N8, Equivalent Fractions) to $\frac{7}{20}$.

EXAMPLE

$0.2079 = \frac{2079}{10000}$

KEY CONCEPTS

To compare values we need to convert them all to the same type: fractions, decimals or percentages

We usually convert to decimals

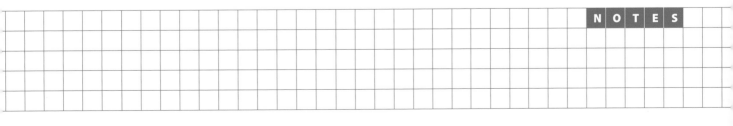

NOTES

REVIEW

1. Convert these fractions to decimals:

    a. $\frac{7}{10}$ b. $\frac{4}{5}$ c. $\frac{5}{8}$ d. $\frac{3}{4}$

2. Convert these percentages to decimals:

    a. 9%   c. 56%

    b. 3%   d. 135%

3. Convert these percentages to fractions:

    a. 5%   c. 20%

    b. 23%   d. 85%

4. Convert these decimals to fractions:

    a. 0·8   c. 0·19

    b. 0·04   d. 0·307

HIGHER PERFORMANCE

1. Convert these fractions to decimals:

    a. $\frac{4}{25}$ b. $\frac{9}{16}$

2. Convert these percentages to decimals:

    a. 12·5%   b. 0·7%

Answers

4. a. $\frac{7}{10} = \frac{4}{5}$ b. $\frac{4}{100} = \frac{1}{25}$ c. $\frac{19}{100}$ d. $\frac{307}{1000}$

3. a. $\frac{5}{100} = \frac{1}{20}$ b. $\frac{23}{100}$ c. $\frac{20}{100} = \frac{1}{5}$ d. $\frac{85}{100} = \frac{17}{20}$

1. a. 0·7   b. 0·8   c. 0·0625   d. 0·75

2. a. 0·9   b. 0·3   c. 0·56   d. 1·35

Answers

1. a. 0·16   b. 0·5625

2. a. 0·125   b. 0·007

NOTES

N12   Ordering of Fractions   N12

'To put fractions in order' means that we have to find the smallest of the fractions, then the next largest, the next largest and so on, to the biggest.

If the fractions all have the same number on the bottom (denominator) then we only have to compare the top numbers (numerators).

EXAMPLE   To put $\frac{5}{7}$, $\frac{2}{7}$ and $\frac{6}{7}$ in order, we notice, first of all, that the bottom numbers (denominators) are all the same. This means that they are all, in this case, sevenths.

Now, we have to put the top numbers in order. The numbers are 5, 2 and 6, so the order (for smallest to largest) is 2, 5, 6. This means that the correct order of the fractions is $\frac{2}{7}$, $\frac{5}{7}$, $\frac{6}{7}$.

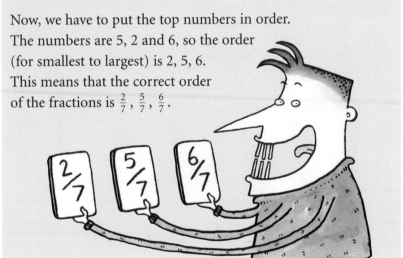

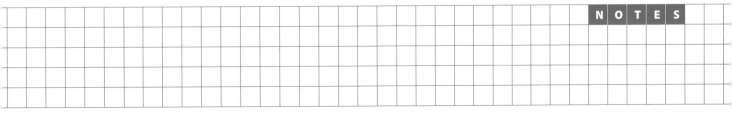

N O T E S

If the fractions do not have the same denominator then we have a little more work to do before we carry out the steps explained above. We need to rewrite the fractions as other, equivalent, fractions (▶ N8, Equivalent Fractions) that all have the same bottom number (denominator).

EXAMPLE Put $\dfrac{3}{4}$, $\dfrac{5}{6}$, $\dfrac{1}{2}$, $\dfrac{2}{3}$ in order.

We need to find equivalent fractions **with the same denominator.**

This means that we have to find a number that 4, 6, 2 and 3 all go into; that is, a number that has 4, 6, 2 and 3 as factors (▶ N5, Multiples, Factors and Prime Numbers). You might think of 48 or 24 or 60 or lots of other numbers. The best one to choose is the smallest. In this case it is 12. (It does not matter if you chose a bigger number like, say 24, as you will still achieve the final correct answer. It just means that you might have to deal with bigger numbers as we convert to equivalent fractions.)

When we have decided upon the denominator for our equivalent fractions we convert each fraction in the list.

$$\frac{3}{4} = \frac{9}{12} \qquad \frac{5}{6} = \frac{10}{12} \qquad \frac{1}{2} = \frac{6}{12} \qquad \frac{2}{3} = \frac{8}{12}$$

SEE N8, EQUIVALENT FRACTIONS, IF YOU NEED HELP WITH THIS

So, our list of fractions becomes

$$\frac{9}{12}, \frac{10}{12}, \frac{6}{12}, \frac{8}{12} \qquad \text{which, in order, becomes} \qquad \frac{6}{12}, \frac{8}{12}, \frac{9}{12}, \frac{10}{12}$$

$$\updownarrow \quad \updownarrow \quad \updownarrow \quad \updownarrow \qquad\qquad\qquad\qquad\qquad\qquad \updownarrow \quad \updownarrow \quad \updownarrow \quad \updownarrow$$

$$\frac{3}{4}, \frac{5}{6}, \frac{1}{2}, \frac{2}{3} \qquad\qquad\qquad\qquad\qquad\qquad\qquad \frac{1}{2}, \frac{2}{3}, \frac{3}{4}, \frac{5}{6}$$

Therefore, the final order is: $\dfrac{1}{2}$, $\dfrac{2}{3}$, $\dfrac{3}{4}$, $\dfrac{5}{6}$.

NOTES

KEY CONCEPTS

✳ If the denominators are the same just put the numerators in order

✳ With different denominators convert to equivalent fractions with the same denominators

✳ For the denominator of the fractions, choose the smallest common multiple of all the denominators

✳ Put the fractions in order of the new numerators, then write as the original fractions for the answer

REVIEW

1. Which is bigger, $\frac{5}{12}$ or $\frac{1}{2}$?

2. Put these fractions in order from smallest to largest:

   a. $\frac{5}{9}, \frac{2}{9}, \frac{4}{9}$

   b. $\frac{3}{10}, \frac{1}{2}, \frac{2}{5}$

   c. $\frac{5}{6}, \frac{2}{3}, \frac{7}{12}$

HIGHER PERFORMANCE

1. Which is bigger, $\frac{3}{8}$ or $\frac{4}{9}$?

2. Which is bigger, $\frac{3}{10}$ or 0·4?

3. Put these fractions in order from smallest to largest: $\frac{3}{4}, \frac{4}{5}, \frac{7}{10}, \frac{1}{2}$

Answers

1. $\frac{1}{2} = \frac{6}{12}$ so $\frac{1}{2}$ is bigger.

2. a. $\frac{2}{9}, \frac{4}{9}, \frac{5}{9}$ b. $\frac{3}{10}, \frac{2}{5}, \frac{1}{2}$ c. $\frac{7}{12}, \frac{2}{3}, \frac{5}{6}$

Answers

1. 0·4

2. $\frac{4}{9}$

3. $\frac{1}{2}, \frac{7}{10}, \frac{3}{4}, \frac{4}{5}$

NOTES

N13 — Fractions of Quantities

When we have to find a fraction of some quantity the simplest type of question is one like 'Find **one**-fifth of something' or 'Find **one**-eighth of something'. To find the answer to these questions we simply divide by a number.

EXAMPLE

To find one-fifth of something, we are just splitting it into five equal parts so we need to divide it by five.

To find one-fifth of 350 we would divide by five:
one-fifth of 350 is 70

To find one-eighth of 72 we would divide by eight:
one-eighth of 72 is 9

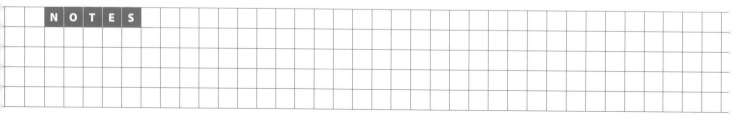

Daily News   15 May, 2000

3/4 of the population have more than one telephone

By Our Reporter

A recent study has shown that more than three-quarters of the
popula... ...enty have more than one telephone, with the

A spokesman said, we estimate that by the year 2005, more
than half of the people su...ed will also have at least three

Nine tenths of the class passed the recent Maths test

N	O	T	E	S																			

A more complicated question would be one where we are asked to find more parts, such as 'Find **four-tenths** of 60'.

To do this, we first find one-tenth, by dividing by ten, and then multiply this answer by four to find the value of four-tenths.

EXAMPLE

To find four-tenths of 60, first find one-tenth of 60:

$60 \div 10 = 6$

Then multiply by 4.

$4 \times 6 = 24$

KEY CONCEPTS

To find $\frac{1}{x}$ of a quantity we divide the quantity by x ✳

To find $\frac{y}{x}$ of a quantity we divide the quantity by x and then multiply the answer by y ✳

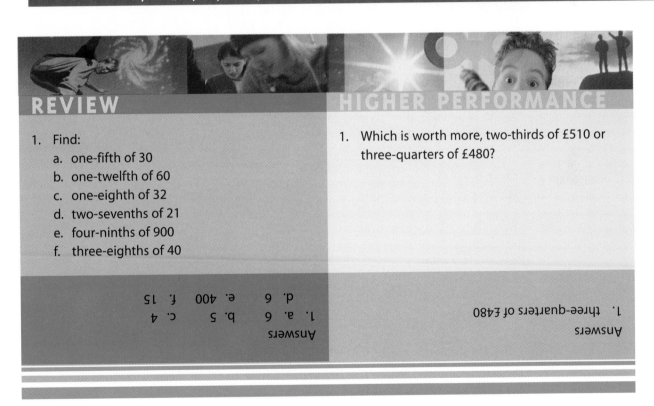

REVIEW

1. Find:
   a. one-fifth of 30
   b. one-twelfth of 60
   c. one-eighth of 32
   d. two-sevenths of 21
   e. four-ninths of 900
   f. three-eighths of 40

HIGHER PERFORMANCE

1. Which is worth more, two-thirds of £510 or three-quarters of £480?

Answers

1. a. 6   b. 5   c. 4
d. 6   e. 400   f. 15

Answers

1. three-quarters of £480

N O T E S

| **N14** | **Simple Addition and Subtraction of Fractions** | **N14** |

	If we add	**kilograms**	to	**kilograms**	we get	**kilograms**
	If we add	**elephants**	to	**elephants**	we get	**elephants**
	If we add	**metres**	to	**metres**	we get	**metres**
	If we add	**fifths**	to	**fifths**	we get	**fifths**

The bottom number of a fraction (denominator) is simply the **unit** (like kilograms or elephants) that we are adding together and so we only need to add the top numbers (numerators).

EXAMPLE

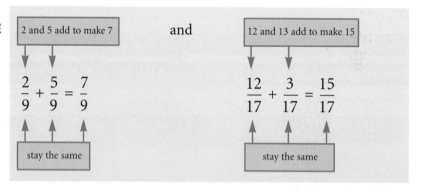

Subtracting is similar.

EXAMPLE

Often, though, the bottom numbers (denominators) are **not** the same numbers. When this happens we have to make them the same by rewriting the fractions as equivalent fractions (▶ N8, Equivalent Fractions) that have the same denominators.

| N O T E S | | | | | | | | | | | | | | | | | | | | | | | | | |

EXAMPLE

$$\frac{1}{6} + \frac{3}{4}$$

The bottom numbers (denominators) are different so we have to rewrite each of the fractions as some other equivalent fraction. What is the smallest number that both 6 and 4 go into? They are both factors of 12, so we will use 12 as the bottom number (denominator) in their equivalent fraction forms.

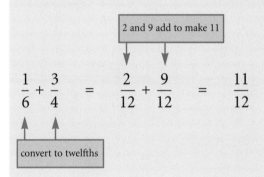

2 and 9 add to make 11

$$\frac{1}{6} + \frac{3}{4} \quad = \quad \frac{2}{12} + \frac{9}{12} \quad = \quad \frac{11}{12}$$

convert to twelfths

Subtracting is similar.

EXAMPLE

$$\frac{3}{5} - \frac{1}{4} \quad = \quad \frac{12}{20} - \frac{5}{20} \quad = \quad \frac{7}{20}$$

Sometimes we need to 'simplify' our final answer.
(▶ See Simplest Form in N8, Equivalent Fractions, if you need help with this.)

EXAMPLE

7 and 2 add to make 9

$$\frac{7}{12} + \frac{1}{6} \quad = \quad \frac{7}{12} + \frac{2}{12} \quad = \quad \frac{9}{12} \quad = \quad \frac{3}{4}$$

÷3

÷3

convert to twelfths

3 divides into 9 and 12

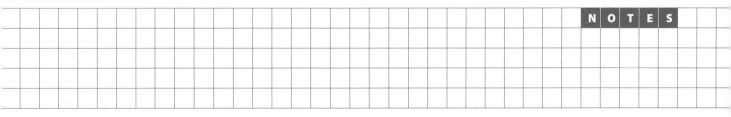

N O T E S

KEY CONCEPTS

✳ If the denominators of the fractions are all the same then simply add (or subtract) the numerators

✳ If the denominators are not the same, first convert to equivalent fractions so that they are

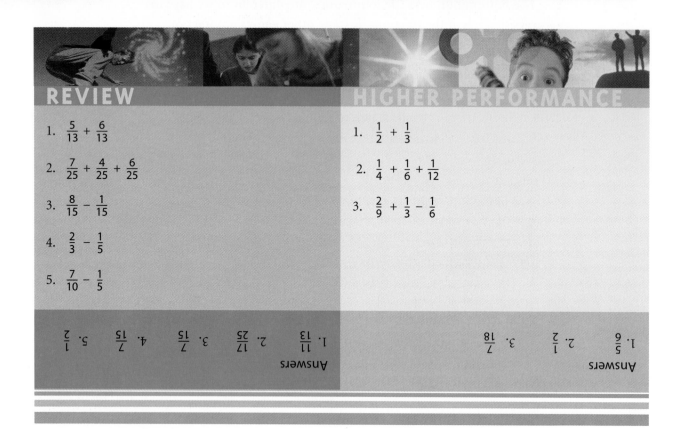

REVIEW

1. $\frac{5}{13} + \frac{6}{13}$

2. $\frac{7}{25} + \frac{4}{25} + \frac{6}{25}$

3. $\frac{8}{15} - \frac{1}{15}$

4. $\frac{2}{3} - \frac{1}{5}$

5. $\frac{7}{10} - \frac{1}{5}$

HIGHER PERFORMANCE

1. $\frac{1}{2} + \frac{1}{3}$

2. $\frac{1}{4} + \frac{1}{6} + \frac{1}{12}$

3. $\frac{2}{9} + \frac{1}{3} - \frac{1}{6}$

Answers

1. $\frac{11}{13}$ 2. $\frac{17}{25}$ 3. $\frac{7}{15}$ 4. $\frac{7}{15}$ 5. $\frac{1}{2}$

Answers

1. $\frac{5}{6}$ 2. $\frac{1}{2}$ 3. $\frac{7}{18}$

N	O	T	E	S																								

Basic Proportion and Ratio

Jamila is redecorating her flat. She wants to paint the walls pink but the paint shop only had pots of red paint and white paint for sale.

She is going to mix some red paint and white paint in a bucket to make some pink paint. The trouble is there are many different shades of pink. She has to be careful to note down how much of each paint colour is used so that when she mixes up some more paint, at another time, it will be exactly the same shade of pink. After some experimenting, Jamila chose to pour three litre tins of white paint and two litre tins of red paint into the large bucket. We say that 'the **ratio** of white to red is 3 to 2' and write this, mathematically, as 3 : 2.

There are, altogether, five litres of paint in the mixture and we say that three-fifths of the mixture is white and two-fifths of the mixture is red. Another way is to say that 'the proportion of white paint is $\frac{3}{5}$' and 'the proportion of red paint is $\frac{2}{5}$'.

We find the total number of parts, which we use for the bottom number of the fraction, by adding together the ratio numbers. In this case we got the 5 from adding the 3 and the 2. Therefore the whole amount is $\frac{3}{5} + \frac{2}{5} = \frac{5}{5} = 1$.
It should always add up to 1.

> WE SAY THAT 'THE RATIO OF WHITE TO RED IS 3 TO 2' AND WRITE THIS, MATHEMATICALLY, AS 3 : 2.

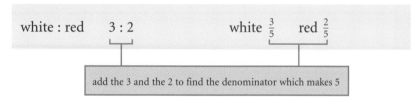

white : red   3 : 2   white $\frac{3}{5}$ red $\frac{2}{5}$

add the 3 and the 2 to find the denominator which makes 5

If Jamila were to mix three litres of white with one litre of red then the ratio of white to red would be 3 : 1.

This would now give a proportion of white paint of $\frac{3}{4}$, and a proportion of red paint of $\frac{1}{4}$. You can check that the fractions are correct as $\frac{3}{4} + \frac{1}{4} = \frac{4}{4} = 1$.

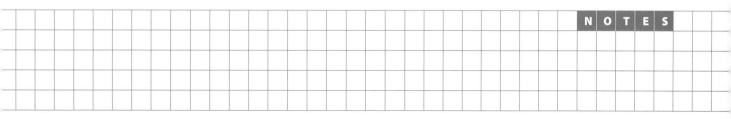

N O T E S

When Ahmed was mixing some concrete he used two bags of cement, four bags of sand and six bags of chippings. For this concrete the ratio of cement to sand to chippings is 2 : 4 : 6. We **could** say that the ratio of chippings to cement to sand is 6 : 2 : 4.

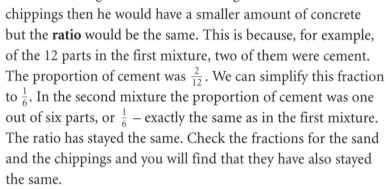

It does not matter what order we use for the numbers provided the **order** of numbers matches the order of the words.

If, instead, Ahmed had used one bag of cement, two bags of sand and three bags of chippings then he would have a smaller amount of concrete but the **ratio** would be the same. This is because, for example, of the 12 parts in the first mixture, two of them were cement. The proportion of cement was $\frac{2}{12}$. We can simplify this fraction to $\frac{1}{6}$. In the second mixture the proportion of cement was one out of six parts, or $\frac{1}{6}$ – exactly the same as in the first mixture. The ratio has stayed the same. Check the fractions for the sand and the chippings and you will find that they have also stayed the same.

So, the ratio 2 : 4 : 6 is the same as the ratio 1 : 2 : 3. In other words, we can simplify ratios, just as we do with fractions, by dividing all of the numbers in the ratio by the **same** value.

THINK ABOUT IT

We can have fractions in ratios, such as $2\frac{1}{2} : 3\frac{1}{2}$. This can be rewritten by multiplying everything by 2 to give 5 : 7.

| N | O | T | E | S |

❋ Using ratios

In a recipe Sam has to mix 1 kg of plain flour with 2 kg of self-raising flour. The ratio of plain flour to self-raising flour is 1 : 2.

Sam has to make 12 kg of this mixture. How much of each type of flour will he use?

First of all Sam needs to work out the total number of parts used. In this mixture there are $1 + 2 = 3$ parts. The plain flour is one of these parts and the self-raising flour is two of the parts. The proportion (or fraction) for plain flour is therefore $\frac{1}{3}$ and for self-raising flour it is $\frac{2}{3}$.

In total there is to be 12 kg. So the plain flour is one-third of the total; that is $12 \div 3 = 4$ kg. The self-raising flour will be two-thirds of the total; that is $12 \div 3 \times 2 = 8$ kg.
We can check our answer by adding the 4 kg and 8 kg to get the total weight of 12 kg.

KEY CONCEPTS

Ratios show us the sizes of the separate parts of something ❋

A proportion is the fraction that a part is of the whole ❋

Ratios can be written in a different form by multiplying or dividing by the same number throughout ❋

N O T E S

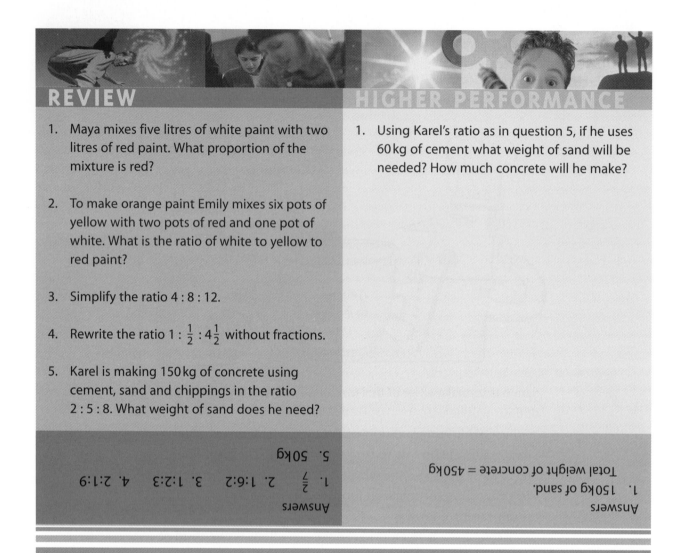

REVIEW

1. Maya mixes five litres of white paint with two litres of red paint. What proportion of the mixture is red?

2. To make orange paint Emily mixes six pots of yellow with two pots of red and one pot of white. What is the ratio of white to yellow to red paint?

3. Simplify the ratio 4 : 8 : 12.

4. Rewrite the ratio $1 : \frac{1}{2} : 4\frac{1}{2}$ without fractions.

5. Karel is making 150 kg of concrete using cement, sand and chippings in the ratio 2 : 5 : 8. What weight of sand does he need?

HIGHER PERFORMANCE

1. Using Karel's ratio as in question 5, if he uses 60 kg of cement what weight of sand will be needed? How much concrete will he make?

Answers

1. $\frac{2}{7}$ 2. 1:6:2   3. 1:2:3   4. 2:1:9

5. 50 kg

Answers

1. 150 kg of sand.
   Total weight of concrete = 450 kg

N16 — Division by Single-digit Numbers with Remainders as Fractions — N16

All of the division sums that we have met so far have had answers that are whole numbers because the number divided **exactly** into the other number without anything left over. Sometimes, though, we have numbers left over. These are called remainders

> NUMBERS LEFT OVER ARE CALLED REMAINDERS

EXAMPLE

When we divide something by, say, 7 we are finding a seventh of the number.

Suppose a group of seven friends go out for a meal at a pizza parlour. They are hungry and ask the chef to bring **all** of the mini pizzas that he has in the kitchen. If the waiter brings a tray of 28 mini pizzas to share between the seven people then, in order to find out how many mini pizzas each person receives, we would have to do the sum 28 ÷ 7.

The answer is 4, so each person would receive four mini pizzas.

Now, suppose that instead of 28 mini pizzas the waiter had brought a tray with 25 mini pizzas on it. The sum that we need to do now is 25 ÷ 7.

Seven goes into 25 three times (that's 21) and there are 4 left over.

The waiter would have given the seven people three mini pizzas each and he would still have four more left on his tray. How would these four pizzas be given out?

The waiter would get a knife and, because there are seven people, he would cut one of the pizzas into seven equal slices. Each slice would be one-seventh of a pizza. He would then give each person one-seventh of a pizza.

The waiter now cuts up another of the left over pizzas into sevenths and gives each person another slice.

He now has two pizzas left on his tray.

He continues to cut up the left over pizzas until they are all gone.

All of the pizzas have now been shared out and there are none left over. Each person received three whole pizzas and also four slices. Remember that each slice was a seventh of a pizza and so we say that each person received $3\frac{4}{7}$ pizzas.
So the new sum, and answer, is written as:

$25 \div 7 = 3\frac{4}{7}$

Because we have divided by 7 then any 'left overs' must each be worth one-seventh.

If we divided by 5 and had some 'left overs' then each one would be one-fifth.

If we divided by 3 and had some 'left overs' then each one would be one-third.

EXAMPLE

Find $47 \div 8$. We find that 8 goes into 47 five times with 7 left over. Each left over is one-eighth, so:

$$47 \div 8 = 5\tfrac{7}{8}$$

Similarly, $48 \div 5$ is 9 with a remainder of 3, so:

$$48 \div 5 = 9\tfrac{3}{5}$$

Sometimes the fraction will need simplifying (as we did in N8, Equivalent Fractions). For example, $26 \div 8 = 3\tfrac{2}{8}$ **but** note that $\tfrac{2}{8} = \tfrac{1}{4}$ so we write:

$$26 \div 8 = 3\tfrac{1}{4}$$

KEY CONCEPTS

The number that we are dividing by tells us the denominator of the fraction for the remainder ✳

The number that is 'left over' tells us the numerator of the fraction for the remainder ✳

N O T E S

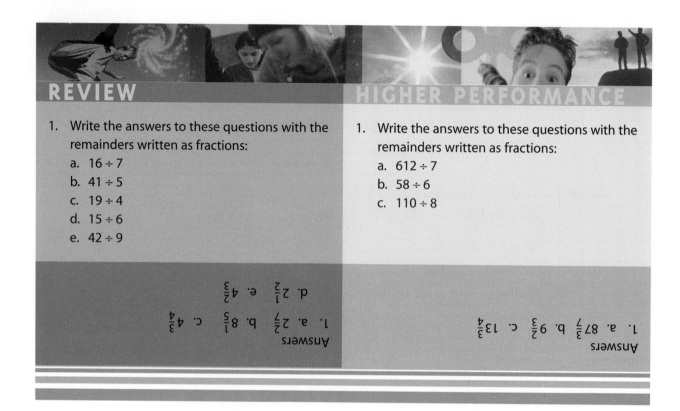

REVIEW

1. Write the answers to these questions with the remainders written as fractions:
    a. $16 \div 7$
    b. $41 \div 5$
    c. $19 \div 4$
    d. $15 \div 6$
    e. $42 \div 9$

Answers

1. a. $2\frac{2}{7}$ b. $8\frac{1}{5}$ c. $4\frac{3}{4}$
d. $2\frac{1}{2}$ e. $4\frac{2}{3}$

HIGHER PERFORMANCE

1. Write the answers to these questions with the remainders written as fractions:
    a. $612 \div 7$
    b. $58 \div 6$
    c. $110 \div 8$

Answers

1. a. $87\frac{3}{7}$ b. $9\frac{2}{3}$ c. $13\frac{3}{4}$

NOTES

N17 | Addition and Subtraction of Decimal Fractions | N17

We met decimal fractions (numbers that have a decimal point in them) in N10, Introduction to Decimal Fractions. We need to be able to add and subtract these sorts of numbers.

EXAMPLE

$23 \cdot 56 + 4 \cdot 92$

$34 \cdot 78 - 16 \cdot 9$

Remember that the decimal point is used to position the digits in the correct columns of tenths, hundredths, thousandths, and so on. This means that in order to add tenths to tenths and hundredths to hundredths, and so on we must put the numbers correctly in line. We use the decimal point to line them up correctly.

EXAMPLE

To start with just ignore the digits – concentrate upon getting the numbers written down **with the decimal points in line.**

So we would write:
$$\begin{array}{r} 23 \cdot 56 \\ + \ 4 \cdot 92 \\ \hline \end{array}$$

Next, put the decimal point in the same place in the answer space:
$$\begin{array}{r} 23 \cdot 56 \\ + \ 4 \cdot 92 \\ \hline \cdot \\ \hline \end{array}$$

Next we add the two numbers just as if there were no decimal point – the decimal point has served its purpose of lining up the numbers ready for adding. The stages leading to our final answer are:

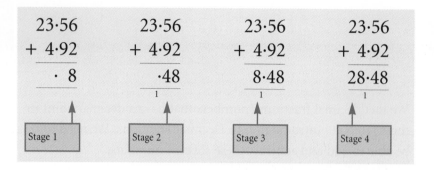

It is the same with subtraction.

EXAMPLE   Find 34·78 − 16·9

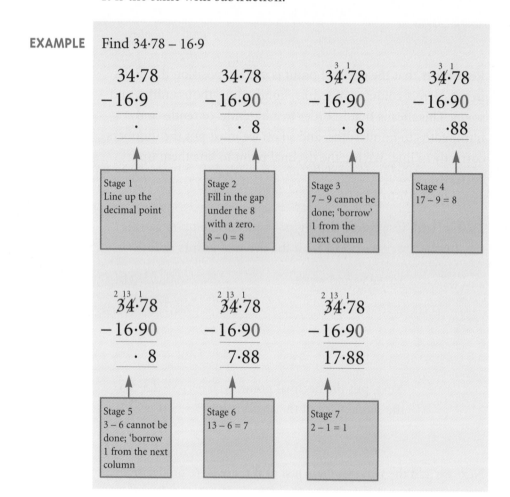

REVIEW

1. 34·69 + 21·7

2. 67·38 – 15·17

3. 45·28 – 2·6

4. 5·97 + 34·28

HIGHER PERFORMANCE

1. 82·41 – 17·8

2. 136·1 – 82·9

3. 56·6 – 20·93

Answers
1. 56·39
2. 52·21
3. 42·68
4. 40·25

Answers
1. 64·61
2. 53·2
3. 35·67

| N18 | Multiplication and Division of Decimal Fractions by 10, 100, 1000 | N18 |

The decimal system uses 10s, 100s, 1000s, and so on and tenths, hundredths, thousandths, and so on, and this makes it very easy to multiply and divide by these numbers.

In N10, Introduction to Decimal Fractions, we saw that the columns in the decimal system are like this:

1000s	100s	10s	1s	•	$\frac{1}{10}$s	$\frac{1}{100}$s	$\frac{1}{1000}$s	$\frac{1}{10000}$s
				•				

Each column is worth ten times more than the column to its right. This means that moving digits to the left, such as moving a 7 in the tenths column to the units column, makes the digit worth ten times more.

1000s	100s	10s	1s	•	$\frac{1}{10}$s	$\frac{1}{100}$s	$\frac{1}{1000}$s	$\frac{1}{10000}$s
			7	•				

Moving the 7 into the next column makes it worth 70 – that is, ten times bigger. And moving it again makes it worth 700 (remember to fill in the gaps with zeros to get the 7 in the correct place).

1000s	100s	10s	1s	•	$\frac{1}{10}$s	$\frac{1}{100}$s	$\frac{1}{1000}$s	$\frac{1}{10000}$s
		7	0	•				
	7	0	0	•				

So to multiply by 10 we move the digits one place to the left. To multiply by 100 we move the digits two places to the left. To multiply by 1000 we move the digits three places to the left, and so on.

NOTES

EXAMPLE $34 \times 100 = 3400$ and $17{\cdot}82 \times 10 = 178{\cdot}2$

Dividing makes the digits worth less and we move them to the right.
So to divide by 10 we move the digits one place to the right.
To divide by 100 we move the digits two places to the right.
To divide by 1000 we move the digits three places to the right, and so on.

1000s	100s	10s	1s	•	$\frac{1}{10}$s	$\frac{1}{100}$s	$\frac{1}{1000}$s	$\frac{1}{10000}$s
			0	•	0	4		

Moving the 4 into the next column makes it ten times smaller.

1000s	100s	10s	1s	•	$\frac{1}{10}$s	$\frac{1}{100}$s	$\frac{1}{1000}$s	$\frac{1}{10000}$s
			0	•	0	0	4	

EXAMPLE $0{\cdot}067 \div 100 = 0{\cdot}000\,67$ and $17{\cdot}82 \div 10 = 1{\cdot}782$

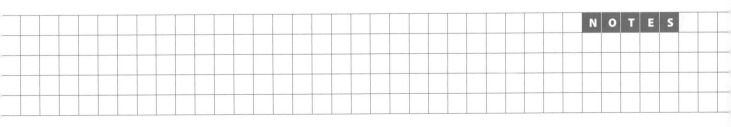

KEY CONCEPTS

Multiplying by 10, 100, 1000, and so on moves the digits to the left (to make the number bigger) ✳

Dividing by 10, 100, 1000, and so on moves the digits to the right (to make the number smaller) ✳

You may need to fill in gaps with zeros to put the digits in the correct columns ✳

NOTES

REVIEW

1. 78×1000

2. $2 \cdot 9413 \times 100$

3. $5403 \cdot 6 \div 100$

4. $0 \cdot 000\,528 \div 10$

Answers
1. 78000　　3. 54·036
2. 294·13　　4. 0·000 0528

HIGHER PERFORMANCE

1. $7 \cdot 8 \times 1000$

2. $0 \cdot 3 \times 100$

3. $0 \cdot 6 \div 100$

4. $0 \cdot 010\,528 \times 100$

Answers
1. 7800　　3. 0·006
2. 30　　　 4. 1·0528

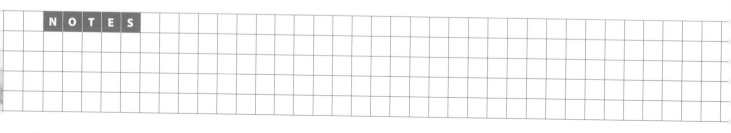

NOTES

| **N19** | **Simple Application of Percentages** | **N19** |

✳ Finding a percentage of something

Finding a percentage of something means finding a fraction of something.

EXAMPLE

A school announced that 40% of its pupils live more than 3 km from the school. In the school there are 600 pupils. How many pupils live more than 3 km from the school?

We need to find 40% of 600 pupils.
40% means $\frac{40}{100}$ (▶ See N9, Introduction to Percentages)
so 40% of 600 means $\frac{40}{100}$ of 600.

Using fractions

Divide 600 by 100 to find that $\frac{1}{100}$ of 600 = 6. So now $\frac{40}{100}$ of 600 means 40 lots of 6 or $40 \times 6 = 240$.

Thus 240 of the 600 pupils live more than 3 km from the school.

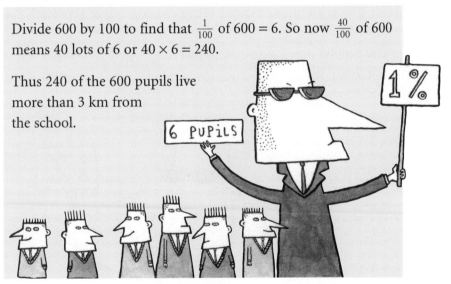

It is useful to have a rough idea of what the answer is likely to be. In this case we know that 40% is less than 50%, so our answer should be less than half of the 600 pupils. Half of 600 is 300, so our answer of 240 is reasonable.

NOTES

Using decimals

Another way of calculating this is to use decimal fractions. In N10, Introduction to Decimal Fractions, we saw that fractions like $\frac{40}{100}$ can be rewritten as $0\cdot40$. To find 40% of 600, we can find $0\cdot40 \times 600$.

$$0\cdot40 \times 600 = 0\cdot40 \times 100 \times 6$$
$$= 40 \times 6$$
$$= 240$$

So we have the same answer as before.

Using 'one percent'

Remember that the 'whole' of the something that we are looking for a percentage of is always 100%.

So the whole school of 600 pupils is 100%.
Now 40% is 40 times 1%, and 1% is a hundredth of 100%.

600 pupils		6 pupils		240 pupils
100%	÷ 100 →	1%	× 40 →	40%

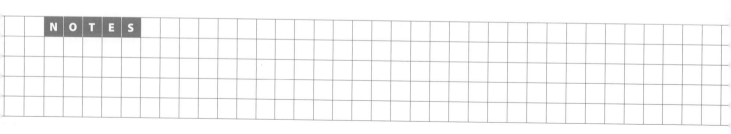

Using a calculator

Sometimes the numbers involved are rather difficult to work with and we have to use a calculator. When this happens we have to carry out the same steps as above but we use a calculator to do the difficult calculations for us.

EXAMPLE

A drying machine removes 32% of the moisture in a piece of clothing. If a shirt has 180 g of water in it before drying, what is the weight of water that the drying machine removes?

We have to find 32% of 180 g.

We can have a rough idea of the answer to expect because 32% is about a third.

So the answer will be about a third of 180.
That is, $180 \div 3 = 60$ g.

Method 1: Using fractions

32% of 180 means $\frac{32}{100} \times 180$.
Divide 180 by 100 to find that $\frac{1}{100}$ of $180 = 180 \div 100 = 1 \cdot 8$.

Now $\frac{32}{100}$ of $180 = 32 \times 1 \cdot 8 = 57 \cdot 6$ (using the calculator).

So the drying machine removes 57.6 g of water.

Method 2: Using decimals

From N9, Introduction to Percentages, we know that
$32\% = 0 \cdot 32$, so 32% of 180 means $0 \cdot 32 \times 180 = 57 \cdot 6$
(using the calculator), as before.

Method 3: Using 'one percent'

First find 1% of $180 = 180 \div 100 = 1 \cdot 8$.
Then to find 32% we multiply this by 32: $1 \cdot 8 \times 32 = 57 \cdot 6$
(using the calculator), as before.

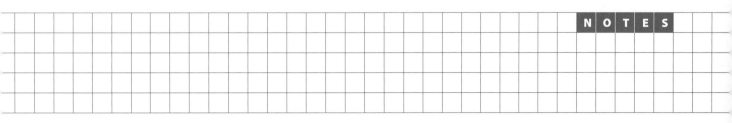

NOTES

KEY CONCEPTS

✳ Finding a percentage of a number means multiplying by a fraction or a decimal

✳ Also find a percentage by finding 1% and then multiplying by the number of per cent required

✳ Do a rough check of your answers

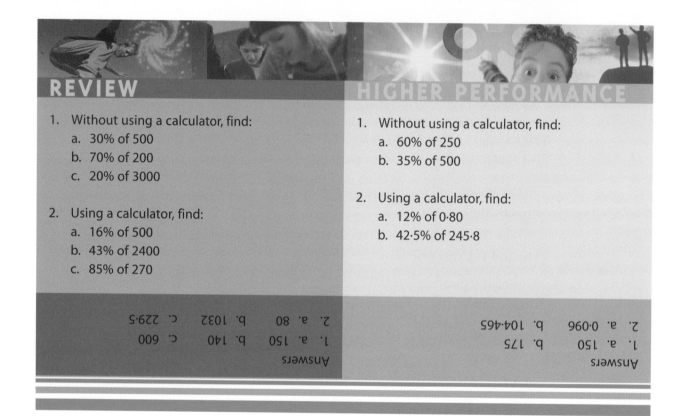

REVIEW

1. Without using a calculator, find:
   a. 30% of 500
   b. 70% of 200
   c. 20% of 3000

2. Using a calculator, find:
   a. 16% of 500
   b. 43% of 2400
   c. 85% of 270

Answers
1. a. 150   b. 140   c. 600
2. a. 80   b. 1032   c. 229·5

HIGHER PERFORMANCE

1. Without using a calculator, find:
   a. 60% of 250
   b. 35% of 500

2. Using a calculator, find:
   a. 12% of 0·80
   b. 42·5% of 245·8

Answers
1. a. 150   b. 175
2. a. 0·096   b. 104·465

N O T E S

N20 Extension of the Number Line to Include Negative Numbers N20

The temperature in some countries in Africa is always warm and it never falls to temperatures like 0°C (zero), when ice would form. In those countries the thermometers for measuring the temperature could start at zero and go up to 50°C.

They would look like this: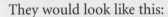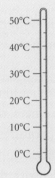

The scale on the thermometer is like a number line, just like the labelling along an axis on a graph.

In other countries, such as countries in Northern Europe, the temperature falls to 0°C and even further sometimes. To show these much lower temperatures we need a number line that goes below 0°C.

Instead of marking on a thermometer, for these temperatures, statements like '1°C below 0°C', '2°C below 0°C', '3°C below 0°C' and so on, we use a negative sign '–' in front of each number.

So, instead of writing '1°C below 0°C', '2°C below 0°C', '3°C below 0°C' and so on, we write '–1°C', '–2°C', '–3°C' and so on.

This means that our thermometer would now look like this:

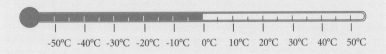

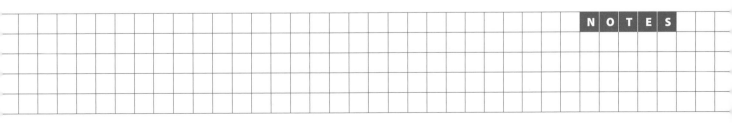

This thermometer is marked in stages of 10°C but a number line is usually marked in stages of 1 unit.

When we are working with a number line it is helpful to have it across the page. Therefore our extended number line would like this:

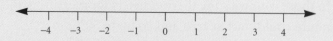

> THE NUMBER LINE EXTENDS TO INFINITY IN BOTH DIRECTIONS

Notice that the line extends in both directions. Mathematicians say it extends to infinity in both directions.

We can use this extended number line to decide which of two numbers is larger. Of two numbers, the one farthest to the **right** is **larger** (or thinking of temperatures, is warmer). Similarly, the one farthest to the **left** is **smaller** (in temperatures this means that it is colder). For example, with the two numbers, 2 and −3, the larger of these two numbers is 2 as it is farther to the right along the number line.

KEY CONCEPTS

✳ Negative numbers are an extension of the number line

✳ Negative numbers are less than zero

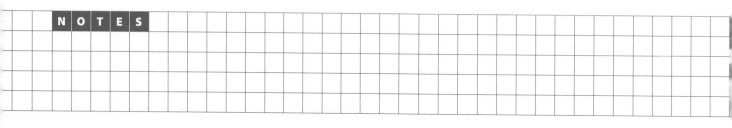

NOTES

REVIEW

1. Which is the larger number in each of these pairs of numbers:
   a. 5 and 12
   b. −3 and 7
   c. −5 and −8
   d. 0 and 6
   e. 0 and −1?

2. Put this list of numbers in order beginning with the lowest:
   13, −4, 0, −10, 3, 4

3. The temperature in Madrid is 21°C, in Strasbourg it is 3°C and in Moscow it is −5°C.
   a. Which place is the hottest?
   b. How many degrees hotter is Madrid than Strasbourg?
   c. How many degrees colder is Moscow than Strasbourg?

HIGHER PERFORMANCE

1. Put each of these sets of numbers in order, beginning with the smallest number:
   a. 6, −4, 0, −1
   b. −5, 3·2, −0·7
   c. 8·01, −9·26, −0·0001

2. The temperature in Oslo is −7°C. Berlin is 6°C warmer and Minsk is 7°C colder.
   a. What is the temperature in Berlin?
   b. What is the temperature in Minsk?

Answers

1. a. 12   b. 7   c. −5   d. 6   e. 0
2. −10, −4, 0, 3, 4, 13
3. a. Madrid   b. 18°C   c. 8°C

Answers

1. a. −4, −1, 0, 6
   b. −5, −0·7, 3·2
   c. −9·26, −0·0001, 8·01
2. a. −1°C
   b. −14°C

All numbers are either positive or negative, except for zero, which is neither.

Think of the number line, which has every number either to the right of zero (positive) or to the left of zero (negative) except for zero itself, which is neither to the left nor to the right.

When writing numbers we should really always show whether they are negative (with a negative sign, like –3) or positive (with a positive sign, like +3). However, in practice we assume that if there is no sign then we mean the value to be a positive value. So 3 means the same as +3.

We must be careful to recognise when the sign '–' means 'negative' and when it means 'take away'. When it is between two numbers, as in 7 – 3 it means 'take away'. If the '–' sign is attached to one number, and **not** between two numbers, it means, 'negative', as in –3. Similarly there is a difference between 'positive 3' as shown by +3, and 'add 3' written as + 3.

A good way to understand this is by thinking of bank accounts. In this situation –3 would mean that you have a **negative** amount in the bank, that is, you **owe** the bank £3; you are **overdrawn** by £3. If you had a balance 'take away 3' then this would mean that you had **taken out** £3 from your bank account. And '+3' would mean that your balance was £3. A balance 'add 3' would mean that you had **paid in** £3 to your account. Some examples of statements using this model of a bank account are:

EXAMPLE

7 – 3   A balance of £7 in the bank take away £3, leaving £4: 7 – 3 = 4

–3   Negative £3 in your bank: you are **overdrawn** by £3

5 + 3   A balance of £5 in the bank and you **add**, or **pay in**, £3, leaving £8 in the account: 5 + 3 = 8

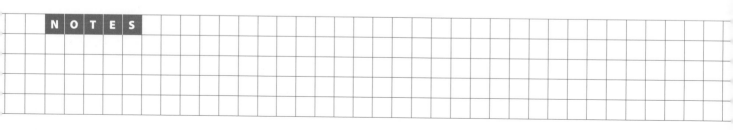

N O T E S

Addition and subtraction with negative numbers

Adding with negative numbers means 'tidying up'. Let's think of a bank again, sorting out how much you actually have in your account after paying money in and taking money out.

EXAMPLE $7 + 4 - 2 + -5 - -3$

In words, this is '7 add 4, take away 2, add negative 5, take away negative 3'. The first part is straightforward with 7 and 4 adding to 11 and then taking away 2, leaving 9, but how do we deal with the **double** signs like $+ -5$ and $- -3$?

In the bank, $+ -5$ means **pay in**, or add to the account, an **overdraft** of £5, which is the same as taking £5 out of the account. So, $+ -5$ means the same as -5. In general, whenever we see '$+ -$' we can rewrite it as '$-$'.

Now $- -3$ means to **take out** of the account an **overdraft** of £3. This is like the bank removing the overdraft from the account. The same result could be achieved by simply paying £3 into the account, so $- -3$ means the same as $+ 3$. In general, whenever we see '$- -$' we can rewrite it as '$+$'. The best way to deal with sums where we have some double signs is to firstly scan the sum replacing any '$+ -$' with '$-$', and any '$- -$' with '$+$'. Doing this with the sum above:

$$7 + 4 - 2 + -5 - -3 \;=\; 7 + 4 - 2 - 5 + 3$$

becomes '$-$'   becomes '$+$'

Now we can continue the sum in the way that we began it, at the start: 7 add 4 gives 11, then take away 2, gives 9, then take away 5, gives 4, then add 3, gives 7.

$$7 + 4 - 2 - 5 + 3 = 7$$

EXAMPLE Similarly, consider the sum: $3 - 2 + -9 + 4 - -1 - 5$

This becomes: $3 - 2 - 9 + 4 + 1 - 5$

That is, 3 take away 2 gives 1, then take away 9, gives –8, then add 4, gives –4, then add 1, gives –3, then take away 5, gives –8.

$$3 - 2 - 9 + 4 + 1 - 5 = -8$$

✳ Multiplication and division with negative numbers

We saw above how to deal with 'double signs' when adding and subtracting.

One rule that people find useful is 'two signs the same means positive: two signs different means negative'.

	Double sign	Is the same as	
Signs the same	– – + +	+ +	Positive
Signs different	– + + –	– –	Negative

The same rule applies when we multiply or divide with two numbers.

EXAMPLE $-3 \times 2 = -6$

The numbers have different signs, so the answer is negative. So since $3 \times 2 = 6$, we have –6 as the answer.

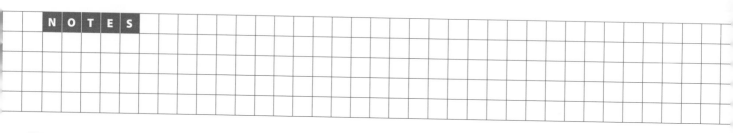

EXAMPLE $-5 \times -4 = 20$

The numbers have the same signs, so the answer is positive. So since $5 \times 4 = 20$, and there is no need to write the + sign, we have 20 as the answer.

KEY CONCEPTS

Tidying up positive and negative numbers is like moving money into and out of a bank account ✳

Double signs have to be made into a single sign using the rule 'two the same = +; two different = –' ✳

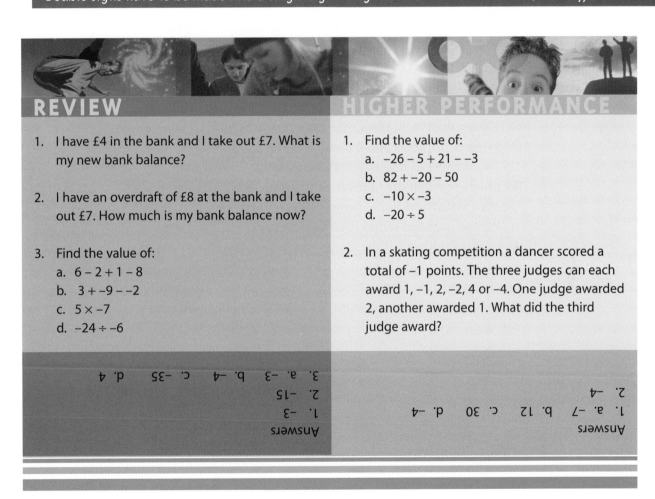

REVIEW

1. I have £4 in the bank and I take out £7. What is my new bank balance?

2. I have an overdraft of £8 at the bank and I take out £7. How much is my bank balance now?

3. Find the value of:
   a. $6 - 2 + 1 - 8$
   b. $3 + -9 - -2$
   c. 5×-7
   d. $-24 \div -6$

Answers
1. –3
2. –15
3. a. –3   b. –4   c. –35   d. 4

HIGHER PERFORMANCE

1. Find the value of:
   a. $-26 - 5 + 21 - -3$
   b. $82 + -20 - 50$
   c. -10×-3
   d. $-20 \div 5$

2. In a skating competition a dancer scored a total of –1 points. The three judges can each award 1, –1, 2, –2, 4 or –4. One judge awarded 2, another awarded 1. What did the third judge award?

Answers
1. a. –7   b. 12   c. 30   d. –4
2. –4

'After 11 years as Manager of Wilsham Rovers I was very disappointed with the team's latest match. In front of a crowd of 4000 fans we could only manage a draw after 90 minutes.'

In this article from a newspaper not all of the values are **exact**. When the manager says that he has been the manager for 11 years he probably means that he has been the manager for **approximately** 11 years. He may have been the manager for more than 11 years but the exact length of time is closer to 11 years than it is to 12 years. If the exact length of time is less than 11 years then he is saying that the length of time is closer to 11 years than to 10 years. (He has actually been the manager for 11 years, 13 weeks and 4 days.)

The number of fans was not **exactly** 4000 – it was 3823 – but the article says that the number was roughly 4000. The number has been **rounded** to the nearest 1000.

We use **rounded** values (that is, not exact values) a great deal. Even the length of the match was not exactly 90 minutes; it was 90 minutes and 47 seconds! The reason why rounded values have been used is to make the article easier to read and, **in this case**, it is not necessary to know the **exact** values involved.

If we did use the exact values then the article would be like this:

> *'After 11 years 13 weeks and 14 days as Manager of Wilsham Rovers I was very disappointed with the team's latest match. In front of a crowd of 3823 fans we could only manage a draw after 90 minutes and 47 seconds.'*

It is not so easy to follow, is it?

The manager was giving the length of time that he had been the manager to the nearest year. The degree of accuracy that he was using was **to the nearest year**. For the number of fans the first article used **to the nearest thousand** as the **degree of accuracy**. The length of the match was given **to the nearest minute** as the **degree of accuracy**.

Sometimes we are told the degree of accuracy being used but other times we have to work it out from the context. For example the statement 'the TV programme lasted 25 minutes' has probably used rounding to the nearest 5 minutes, or possibly to the nearest minute. We certainly do not expect this value to be given to the nearest second.

It always depends upon how we are going to use the values. Is it to gain an understanding of the approximate amount involved or is it needed for a very precise and accurate piece of work? For example, the value 1 246 473 could be the population of Montevideo or it could be a phone number. In most situations, for the population of Montevideo, it would be acceptable to use a degree of accuracy of the nearest thousand, so we would say, 'The population of Montevideo is 1 246 000'. For the phone number, we need this value to be given **exactly** if we are to make use of it and so we would say, 'The phone number that you need is 1246473'.

When we have a number made up from several digits and we are going to **round** the number, we are going to lose some of the information in the number. We need to keep the most important parts of the number. Another word for 'important' is '**significant**'. In the statement 'the population of Montevideo is 1 246 473' the most significant (important) figure (digit) is the '1' that stands for one million. The second **significant figure** is the '2' that stands for two hundred thousand. The '4' is the third **significant figure** and so on until we reach the '3', which is the seventh **significant figure**. We often abbreviate **significant figure** to sig. fig. or s.f.

In the article about the football match the value 4000 would be the value of 3823 given to one significant figure. To decide what the value is to 1 sig. fig. we recognise firstly that 3823 is a value that lies between 3000 and 4000. We simply have to decide which of these it is closest to.

Imagine a scale, like on a ruler, to show this:

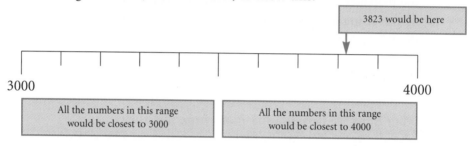

We can see that 3823 is closest to 4000. We do not need a diagram to work this out.

When we are allowed only 1 sig. fig. we must look at the next most important figure, the one that we are going to 'chop off'. In this case it is 8. The dividing line between 3000 and 4000 is at 3500. If the digit we are chopping off is below 5 the number is below 3500 and therefore closer to 3000 (we round **down**). If the digit that is going to be chopped off is above 5 the number is above 3500 and therefore closer to 4000 (we round **up**). If the number we are going to chop off is exactly 5 we are generous and round **up**.

EXAMPLE   If we were to round the number of the people at the football match to 2 sig. fig. we would work out the answer like this:

3823 lies between 3800 and 3900 (remember that we are using the first **two** most important, **significant**, digits). We are chopping off the third digit, 2, which is less than 5, so we are closer to 3800.

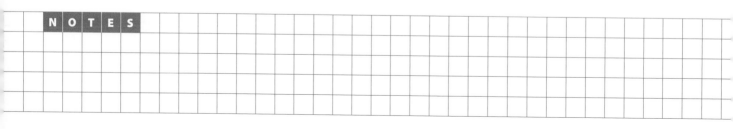

EXAMPLE   Find 1 246 473 rounded to 3 sig. fig.

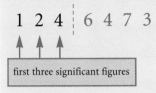

first three significant figures

Our answer is either 1 240 000 or 1 250 000. Because 6 is more than 5 (we are **over** halfway) we are closer to 1 250 000.

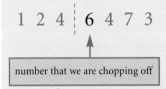

number that we are chopping off

So, 1 246 473 = 1 250 000 to 3 sig. fig.

The first significant figure of a number is the one that is furthest to the left, because it is worth more than any other digit. Remember that the further to the left we move, the higher value each column has. This is still true with columns that are fractions, that is, to the right of the decimal point.

EXAMPLE

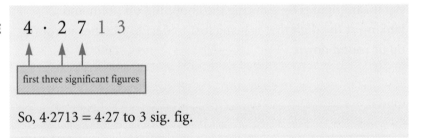

first three significant figures

So, 4·2713 = 4·27 to 3 sig. fig.

Be careful, with decimal fractions starting with zero, because the first digit on the left is not the first significant figure. For example, in the number 0·000 841 3 the first significant figure is the 8 because the zeros to the left of the 8 are **not** important (significant); they are just there to push the 8 into the correct column. They are used to space out the number correctly.

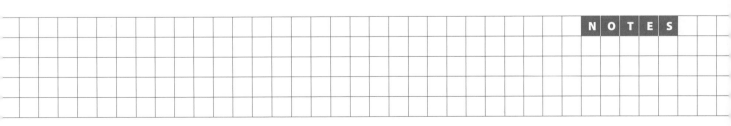

N O T E S

EXAMPLE

$$0 \cdot 0 \ 0 \ 0 \ 8 \ 4 \ 1 \ 3$$

1st 2nd 3rd significant figures

So, 0·000 841 3 = 0·000 84 to 2 sig. fig.

or 0·000 841 3 = 0·000 841 to 3 sig. fig. and so on.

Sometimes the degree of accuracy is given as so many **decimal places**, (which can be abbreviated to **dec. pl.** or **d.p.**).

EXAMPLE

$$1 \ 4 \cdot 5 \ 3 \ 9$$

1st 2nd 3rd significant figures

So, 14·539 = 14·5 to 1 d.p.

or 14·539 = 14·54 to 2 d.p. and so on.

So for decimal places we use the same principles as for significant figures by marking the chopping off point and looking at the digit that is being lost to decide whether to round up or round down.

KEY CONCEPTS

✳ Draw a line after the significant figure or decimal place where you are going to 'chop'

✳ Look at the number that you will chop off

✳ If it is below 5 round down (leave the numbers before the chopping off line as they are)

✳ If it is 5 or above round up (add one to the last number before the chopping off line)

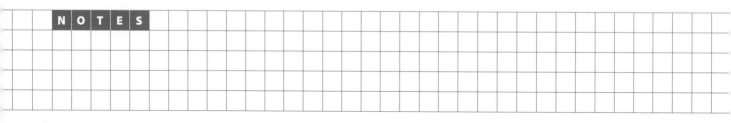

N O T E S

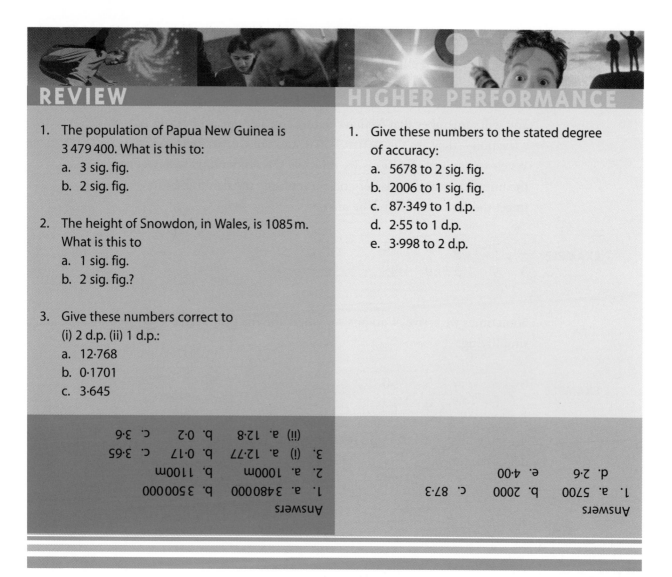

REVIEW

1. The population of Papua New Guinea is 3 479 400. What is this to:
    a. 3 sig. fig.
    b. 2 sig. fig.

2. The height of Snowdon, in Wales, is 1085 m. What is this to
    a. 1 sig. fig.
    b. 2 sig. fig.?

3. Give these numbers correct to
    (i) 2 d.p. (ii) 1 d.p.:
    a. 12·768
    b. 0·1701
    c. 3·645

HIGHER PERFORMANCE

1. Give these numbers to the stated degree of accuracy:
    a. 5678 to 2 sig. fig.
    b. 2006 to 1 sig. fig.
    c. 87·349 to 1 d.p.
    d. 2·55 to 1 d.p.
    e. 3·998 to 2 d.p.

Answers

1. a. 3 480 000   b. 3 500 000
2. a. 1000 m   b. 1100 m
3. (i) a. 12·77   b. 0·17   c. 3·65
   (ii) a. 12·8   b. 0·2   c. 3·6

Answers

1. a. 5700   b. 2000   c. 87·3
   d. 2·6   e. 4·00

| N23 | **Simple Multiplication of Vulgar Fractions** | N23 |

You will remember that we have names for the top and bottom of a fraction – they are the **numerator** and the **denominator**. When we multiply fractions we multiply the numerators to get the numerator in the answer and we multiply the denominators to get the denominator in the answer.

EXAMPLE
$$\frac{2}{5} \times \frac{7}{9} = \frac{2}{5} \times \frac{7}{9} = \frac{14}{45}$$

Sometimes we arrive at an answer where the fraction needs simplifying.

EXAMPLE
$$\frac{6}{7} \times \frac{5}{9} = \frac{6 \times 5}{7 \times 9} = \frac{30}{63}$$

We know that 3 divides into both the numerator and denominator.

$$\frac{30}{63} = \frac{10}{21}$$

So $\frac{10}{21}$ is the final simplified answer.

We can avoid this process of looking for a number that divides into the numerator and denominator in order to simplify the fraction by simplifying it **before** we start.

NOTES

EXAMPLE Looking at the question $\frac{6}{7} \times \frac{5}{9}$ we need to look for a number that divides into **any** number on the top but that also divides into a number on the bottom.

Here we should see that the 6 on the top and the 9 on the bottom can both be divided by 3.

We simplify the question (rather than simplifying the answer at the end) by dividing 3 into these numbers.

We set it out like this: $\dfrac{\overset{2}{\cancel{6}}}{7} \times \dfrac{5}{\underset{3}{\cancel{9}}}$

which gives us $\dfrac{2 \times 5}{7 \times 3} = \dfrac{10}{21}$

The process of reducing the 6 to a 2 (and the 9 to a 3) is sometimes called **cancelling**. Cancelling can sometimes save us a great deal of work in trying to simplify a fraction at the end.

EXAMPLE $\dfrac{14}{15} \times \dfrac{3}{7} = \dfrac{\overset{2}{\cancel{14}}}{15} \times \dfrac{3}{\underset{1}{\cancel{7}}} = \dfrac{\overset{2}{\cancel{14}}}{\underset{5}{\cancel{15}}} \times \dfrac{\overset{1}{\cancel{3}}}{\underset{1}{\cancel{7}}} = \dfrac{2 \times 1}{5 \times 1} = \dfrac{2}{5}$

Notice that both 14 and 7 can be divided, by 7

Notice that both 3 and 15 can be divided, by 3

If we had not simplified first then we would have had $\frac{42}{105}$ and it may have taken us longer to find numbers that divided into both 42 and 105, in order to simplify the answer to the final answer of $\frac{2}{5}$.

KEY CONCEPTS

✳ Simplify by finding common factors of numerators and denominators

✳ Cancel common factors wherever possible

✳ Multiply numerators and denominators to get the answer

We can use the same method even if we are multiplying more than just two fractions at a time.

EXAMPLE

$$\frac{14}{25} \times \frac{9}{28} \times \frac{5}{6} = \frac{14}{{}_{5}25} \times \frac{9}{28} \times \frac{\overset{1}{\cancel{5}}}{6}$$

⟵ 5 will go into the 5 and the 25

$$= \frac{14}{{}_{5}25} \times \frac{\overset{3}{\cancel{9}}}{28} \times \frac{\overset{1}{\cancel{5}}}{{}_{2}\cancel{6}}$$

⟵ 3 will go into the 9 and the 6

$$= \frac{\overset{2}{\cancel{14}}}{{}_{5}25} \times \frac{\overset{3}{\cancel{9}}}{{}_{4}\cancel{28}} \times \frac{\overset{1}{\cancel{5}}}{{}_{2}\cancel{6}}$$

⟵ 7 will go into the 14 and the 28

$$= \frac{\overset{\overset{1}{\cancel{2}}}{\cancel{14}}}{{}_{5}25} \times \frac{\overset{3}{\cancel{9}}}{{}_{2}{}_{4}\cancel{28}} \times \frac{\overset{1}{\cancel{5}}}{{}_{2}\cancel{6}}$$

⟵ 2 will go into the 2 on the top and the 4 on the bottom

$$= \frac{1 \times 3 \times 1}{5 \times 2 \times 2} = \frac{3}{20}$$

Without cancelling we would have been looking for numbers that divide into some pretty large numbers!

N	O	T	E	S																		

REVIEW

1. Find the value of:

   a. $\frac{2}{7} \times \frac{3}{5}$

   b. $\frac{21}{25} \times \frac{15}{28}$

   c. $\frac{63}{64} \times \frac{16}{45}$

Answers

1. a. $\frac{6}{35}$

   b. $\frac{9}{20}$

   c. $\frac{7}{20}$

HIGHER PERFORMANCE

1. Find the value of:

   a. $\frac{12}{35} \times \frac{14}{27}$

   b. $\frac{18}{25} \times \frac{14}{27} \times \frac{30}{49}$

Answers

1. a. $\frac{8}{45}$

   b. $\frac{8}{35}$

NOTES

| N24 | **Multiplication and Division of Decimal Fractions by Single-digit Numbers** | N24 |

Multiplying decimal fractions by a single digit (a number between 1 and 9) is very much like multiplying a whole number by a single digit – we just need to make sure that the decimal point is put in the correct place. Consider a sum **without** a decimal point, like 26×7.

EXAMPLE

We set the sum out like this:

$$\begin{array}{r} 2\,6 \\ \times\ 7 \\ \hline \end{array}$$

First we do 7×6:

$$\begin{array}{r} 2\,6 \\ \times\ 7 \\ \hline 2 \\ \scriptstyle 4 \end{array}$$

Then 7×2:

$$\begin{array}{r} 2\,6 \\ \times\ 7 \\ \hline 1\,8\,2 \\ \scriptstyle 4 \end{array}$$

The answer is 182.

Now consider a similar sum but one that has a decimal point in the number, like $2 \cdot 6 \times 7$.

EXAMPLE   We set the sum out, just as before, like this:

$$\begin{array}{r} 2{\cdot}6 \\ \times\ 7 \\ \hline \end{array}$$

First we do 7×6:

$$\begin{array}{r} 2{\cdot}6 \\ \times\ 7 \\ \hline 2 \\ {}_4 \end{array}$$

Next, we come across the decimal point.
We just copy it on to the answer line:

$$\begin{array}{r} 2{\cdot}6 \\ \times\ 7 \\ \hline {\cdot}2 \\ {}_4 \end{array}$$

Finally, we complete the sum as above:

$$\begin{array}{r} 2{\cdot}6 \\ \times\ 7 \\ \hline 18{\cdot}2 \\ {}_4 \end{array}$$

The answer is 18·2.

Remember to check with an estimate: 2·6 is between 2 and 3,
so $7 \times 2{\cdot}6$ must lie between $7 \times 2 = 14$ and $7 \times 3 = 21$.
Our answer does!

EXAMPLE

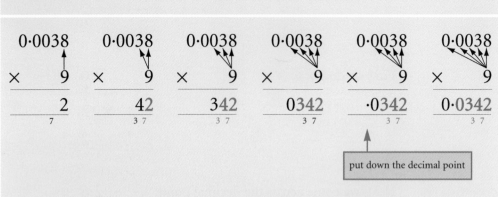

put down the decimal point

Find 0·0038 × 9.

Estimating, we note that 0·0038 is near to 0·004, and 0·004 × 9 = 0·036,

which is near to our answer of 0·0342.

Division is similar because, once again, as we come across the

EXAMPLE decimal point, we just put it into our answer.

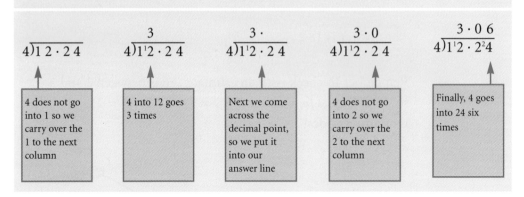

| 4 does not go into 1 so we carry over the 1 to the next column | 4 into 12 goes 3 times | Next we come across the decimal point, so we put it into our answer line | 4 does not go into 2 so we carry over the 2 to the next column | Finally, 4 goes into 24 six times |

We set the sum   12·24 ÷ 4 out like this:

Sometimes we need to add on extra zeros in order to complete the working out. Look back at N11, Equivalence Between Fractions, Percentages and Decimals, to review when we need to do this.

EXAMPLE Find 137 ÷ 4:

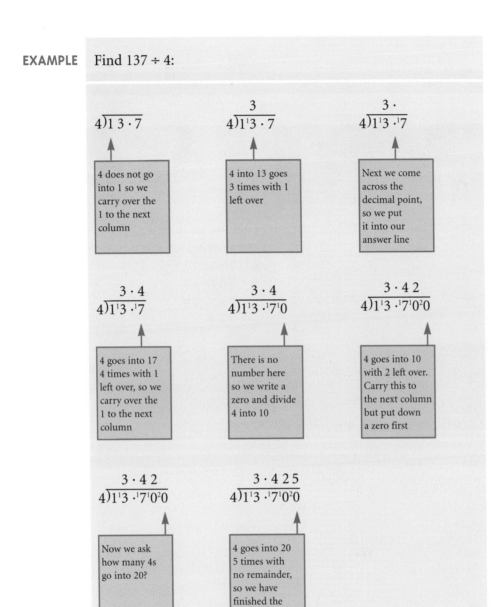

giving the answer 3·425

Using estimation as a check we note that 12 ÷ 4 gives 3 and as 13·7 is close to 12 then we would expect our answer to be close to 3.

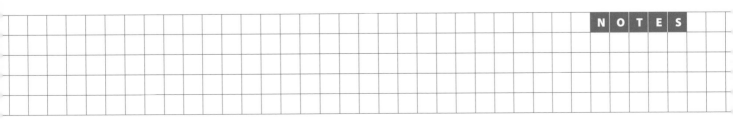

KEY CONCEPTS

✳ Multiply and divide as normal, remembering to put the decimal point in the answer line

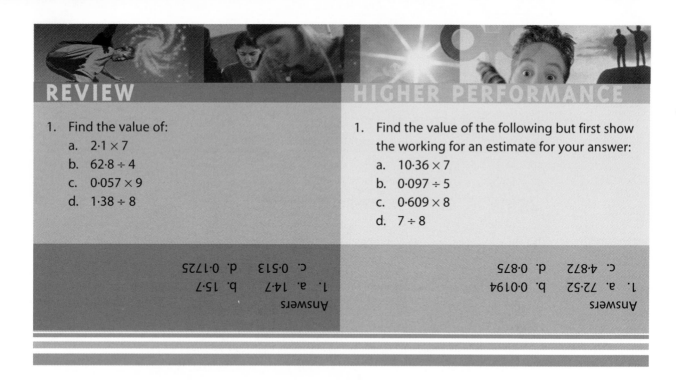

REVIEW

1. Find the value of:
   a. $2·1 \times 7$
   b. $62·8 \div 4$
   c. $0·057 \times 9$
   d. $1·38 \div 8$

Answers
1. a. 14·7   b. 15·7
c. 0·513   d. 0·1725

HIGHER PERFORMANCE

1. Find the value of the following but first show the working for an estimate for your answer:
   a. $10·36 \times 7$
   b. $0·097 \div 5$
   c. $0·609 \times 8$
   d. $7 \div 8$

Answers
1. a. 72·52   b. 0·0194
c. 4·872   d. 0·875

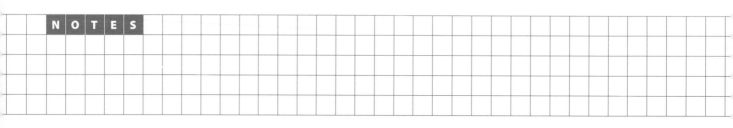

N O T E S

N25 — Multiplication of Decimal Fractions by Decimal Fractions — N25

In N24, Multiplication and Division of Decimal Fractions by Single-digit Numbers, we saw how to multiply a decimal fraction by a whole number. In this chapter we will see how to multiply a decimal fraction by another decimal fraction; that is, how to multiply a number with a decimal point in it by another number with a decimal point in it. An example is the sum 4.7×2.3. It would be helpful to look again at what we did in N3, Multiplication of Whole Numbers by Two-digit Numbers, when we multiplied numbers by two-digit numbers.

We start to calculate the answer by **ignoring** the decimal point – think of the sum as 47×23. We can calculate this as we did in N3, Multiplication of Whole Numbers by Two-digit Numbers, achieving the answer 1081. To complete the answer we now take account of the decimal point. **For every decimal place in the question there must be a decimal place in the answer.** In the sum 4.7×2.3 we have two decimal places, altogether (the 7 and the 3), so we must have two decimal places in our answer. This means that we count two places from the right and put the decimal point into the answer between the 0 and the 8.

> FOR EVERY DECIMAL PLACE IN THE QUESTION THERE MUST BE ONE IN THE ANSWER

EXAMPLE Find 4.7×2.3.

Step 1:	Ignore the decimal point; $47 \times 23 = 1081$
Step 2:	Count the decimal places in the question; here we have two (3 and 7)
Step 3:	Put this many decimal places into the answer, by placing the decimal point accordingly: 10.81 (two decimal places)

A useful step to include is to **estimate** the answer in order to check if it is reasonable.

In this example 4·7 is roughly 5 (it is closer to 5 than it is to 4 – ▶ see N22, Degrees of Accuracy – Significant Figures and Decimal Places) and 2·3 is roughly 2, so our estimation is found by saying 5 × 2 = 10: our answer is close to this. This is not a guarantee that we have the correct answer but it should show us if we have put the decimal point in the wrong place because then we would be very different from the estimate.

When we estimate we have to do the estimate calculation in our head so it should not be too complicated. For this reason we estimate by using each value correct to only 1 sig. fig. (▶ see N22, Degrees of Accuracy – Significant Figures and Decimal Places).

We use the same method if we have only one digit in the number that we are multiplying by.

EXAMPLE   Find 9·3 × 0·8.

Step 1:   Estimate 9·3 × 0·8 as 9 × 1 = 9; our answer should be close to 9

Step 2:   Ignore the decimal points; this gives 93 × 8 = 744

Step 3:   Count the decimal places in the question; we have two (3 and 8)

Step 4:   Put the decimal point in the answer to create the same number of decimal places; 7·44

Step 5:   Compare this with the estimate; yes, it is near to 9

EXAMPLE   Find 7·6 × 0·58.

Step 1:   Estimate 7·6 × 0·58 as 8 × 0·6 = 4·8; our answer should be close to 4·8

Step 2:   Ignore the decimal points; this gives 76 × 58 = 4408

Step 3:   Count the decimal places in the question; we have three (6, 5 and 8)

Step 4:   Put the decimal point in the answer to create the same number of decimal places; 4·408

Step 5:   Compare this with the estimate; yes, it is near to 4·8

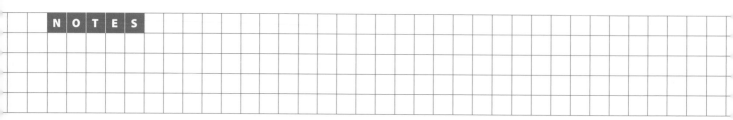

N O T E S

Estimate the answer (use values correct to 1 sig. fig.) ✳

Do the multiplication without any decimal points in the question ✳

Count the number of decimal places needed in the answer ✳

Put the decimal point in the answer in order to create the correct number of decimal places ✳

Check the answer with the estimate ✳

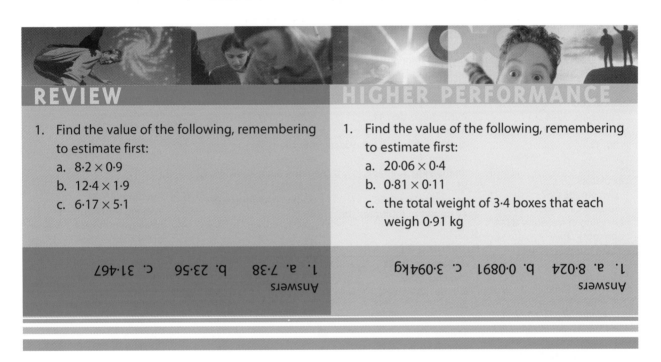

REVIEW

1. Find the value of the following, remembering to estimate first:
   a. $8 \cdot 2 \times 0 \cdot 9$
   b. $12 \cdot 4 \times 1 \cdot 9$
   c. $6 \cdot 17 \times 5 \cdot 1$

Answers
1. a. 7·38   b. 23·56   c. 31·467

HIGHER PERFORMANCE

1. Find the value of the following, remembering to estimate first:
   a. $20 \cdot 06 \times 0 \cdot 4$
   b. $0 \cdot 81 \times 0 \cdot 11$
   c. the total weight of 3·4 boxes that each weigh 0·91 kg

Answers
1. a. 8·024   b. 0·0891   c. 3·094kg

N O T E S

Index